I0006551

The

Ultimate Guide

To Writing

Scientific Theses

Using Word 2007

© 2010 by Dr. Sven Enterlein

All rights reserved.

This book only be distributed through academia-nutcrackers.com or its authorized affiliates. If you like this book please spread the word and leave feedback at www.academia-nutcrackers.com

The bonus archive can be downloaded after registering at www.academia-nutcrackers.com/downloads. The electronic version of this book can be purchased at a discounted price. Please visit the members' area on our website for details.

This book may not be reproduced, in whole or in part, including illustrations, in any form (beyond that copying permitted by Sections 107 and 108 of the U.S. Copyright Law and except by reviewers for the public press), without written permission from the publisher.

Users wishing to use the material in this book for commercial purposes may contact me at support@academia-nutcrackers.com to negotiate suitable arrangements.

All writing, layout, and graphics design by Dr. Sven Enterlein.

Images purchased through ImageEnvision.com. All images used are royalty-free for use by the author.

ISBN 978-0-615-42383-8

Table of Contents

Introduction

First I would like to thank you for your interest in this book. I invested a lot of time and effort to put together a guide that I hope will help students to master the final hurdle of their hard labor: The Thesis.

Not only have I myself been there twice. Many of my friends and coworkers approached me with questions regarding the use of Microsoft Word, Excel, PowerPoint, and other commonly used software when they saw that I *enjoyed* solving the encountered problems. Soon I realized that many questions were rather similar and I became quite proficient in answering them. Even now in my current job as a scientist I am still the point of contact for questions related to all kinds of software and, to a lesser extent, hardware problems.

This led to the idea to compile a comprehensive handbook that does not only deal with the individual features of the programs one at a time but to also answer specific questions explicitly. Obviously, the scope of my work is not to substitute for any already existing, detailed manual but rather pick out the essentials and apply them to a more or less specific problem.

The average path of a (graduate) student is:

    I.   Attend lectures and courses (learn)

    II.   Get hands-on experience in the lab (apply the learned and collect data)

    III.   Analyze the data and make sense of it (data evaluation)

    IV.   Read reference publications (discuss and deepen knowledge)

    V.   (repeat as I-IV often as necessary)

    VI.   Finally, the whole story needs to be wrapped up in a bound document, The Thesis.

For many students that I have met the last step seems to be the hardest and the one most students procrastinate with. In my opinion, writing the thesis should be *exciting* as it is the final step to earning the degree! To present the world with the achievements of the past year(s)! And this is where this guide is intended to help: to ease some of the struggle that writing this final piece of documentation brings.

I sincerely hope that I created a little helper that made your life easier. For updated video tutorials visit 🛈 www.academia-nutcrackers.com/videos.

Warm regards and all the best for the future!

Index of Common Problems

This index is supposed to help you find answers to common problems quickly. It is actually a collection of Frequently Asked Questions. Since many problems are multi-facetted I decided to list the problem and then refer to the pieces of the puzzle within this book that will help you address the question. If you have additional questions that you would like me to add in future revisions I encourage you to send me an email to support@academia-nutcrackers.com or use the contact form on our website (✪ www.academia-nutcrackers.com/contact-form).

Frequently Asked Questions

> **Q: I want to insert a page with a different orientation into my document. Is there an easy way to do that?**

> A: Yes, it is very simple in fact. All that you need to know is how to work with ☞ sections. Check out ☞ *FAQ 1 – How To Insert A Single Landscape Page* for detailed information.

> **Q: Is there anything I can do to structure my document so that I have a properly formatted hierarchy for my headings? Can I use that for my Table of Contents as well?**

> A: You have come to the right place! *FAQ 3 – Structure Your Headings With A Multilevel List* describes exactly that! It can be done with a few clicks if you are happy with the pre-defined formats that Word 2007 offers.

> **Q: Can I customize the headers for each chapter? I would like to include the chapter heading in the header.**

> A: Of course! This requires a bit of attention though. First, you have to familiarize yourself with ☞ styles, ☞ sections and ☞ cross-references. Then you can go to ☞ *FAQ 2 – Customize Headers and Footers* where each step is explained.

> **Q: I sometimes have trouble with the way copy&paste works in Word. Can I control that function and decide how I want items to be inserted?**

> A: Microsoft Office programs are very flexible when it comes to pasting items out of the Clipboard, where everything is stored during copy&paste. Since I feel that a lot of time is wasted not fully taking advantage of the paste feature I listed a few general considerations in ☞ *FAQ 7 – How And What To Paste*

Q: I am really tired that my text elements never align correctly. What can I do?

A: Use ☞ tab stops! In my opinion tab stops are badly underused. They can come in handy not only to align text in different paragraphs but also to align text with graphics. A good example is ☞ *FAQ 9 – Elaborate Tabs: How To Label A Gel Picture.*

Q: Why do the graphics that I insert into my document never stay where they are supposed to be?

A: This is most likely caused by the way the graphic is anchored to the text. If not already enabled press `ctrl+*` to enable formatting symbols. Now read the chapter on ☞ Images, Graphics, Objects & Co. carefully and refer to ☞ *FAQ 5 – Make Objects And Text Play Together Nicely* for a detailed analysis. After that you should be able to tame one of the oldest scourges in Word!

Q: I want to create a numbered list but I would like to be more flexible with my formatting than the regular numbered list option. What can I do?

A: I am happy to tell you that I had the exact same problem when writing Standard Operating Procedures (SOPs): Each step had to get its own number but the actual instructions for each step were very complex. For that reason I utilized a ☞ table in which I formatted one row to contain the numbers and placed the content in the next column. The steps can be found in ☞ *FAQ 4 – Table With Automatic Numbering.*

Q: I heard you can sort of automate the captions for figures or tables. There must be a better way than labeling them all by hand, right?

A: Absolutely! ☞ *FAQ 6 – Adding Text (Captions) To Figures, Tables, etc.* deals with this very important feature of Word. Although it has been available for a long time not everyone is aware of its existence or thinks it's too tedious to use.

Q: I am not finished with my thesis but I want to refer to figures and other chapters within my document. I don't want to manually type all the references because many of them will change and I am sure I will fail to update all of them. What solution does Word 2007 offer?

A: Fortunately, you will be able to refer to virtually anything that is part of your document be it figures, tables, chapters, or even ☞ bookmarks that you set. For everything that is not text (e.g. tables and figures) you will have to create a ☞ caption before you can refer to it. I dedicated an entire chapter to ☞ Cross-References because in my opinion the more dynamic you make your document the better! Make sure to read ☞ *FAQ 8 – How To Insert a Cross-Reference*!

How to Use This Guide

Scope of This Book

I dare to assume that one of the reasons you decided to buy (or otherwise acquire) this book was because you think it can help you with writing your thesis. I think or at least hope so, too!

Here is what I will talk about:

- *Recommendations and preparations.* I'll briefly touch upon what I think might help writing a thesis – Software, hardware, and more.
- *Office 2007.* There have been quite significant changes to the whole Microsoft Office 2007 package compared to older versions. Get used to them – they aren't half as bad as they might appear!
- *Word features.* How can I build a solid Word document? The most important features will be explained. This is the core of this book.
- *Thesis structure.* Most likely you have to follow your institution's guidelines but I still wanted to say a few words of my own.
- *PDF.* The best way to publish a document these days. Some advice will be offered on how to convert a Word document into a PDF.

Additionally, I will include a table with the most commonly used and very handy short-cuts (☞ Using the Keyboard). Over time and with upcoming revisions I will list software and literature references. For now check out the online version at 🌍 http://academia-nutcrackers.com/affiliates-sponsors.

Where is This Book Different?

Well, I don't pretend I reinvented the wheel. The main intention for writing this book was to help students find quick help with Word 2007 when they need it. I did not want to write another Missing Manual or Referendum. There are already tons of great books out there! Where I hope my niche is by answering specific questions quickly. Go to the Index to see what you can learn! Whenever refer to the bonus archive – it can be downloaded after registering at www.academia-nutcrackers.com/downloads.

Design of This Book

Fonts and Formatting

I was wondering and pondering for a while whether to use different fonts when referring to different actions. I decided "yes".

- "Microsoft Sans Serif":   Indicates that a menu option needs to be selected.
- "Courier New":   Corresponds to typing something on the keyboard.

Apart from that everything is formatted in "Garamond" (main text) and "Verdana" (headings).

Icons

Icons don't only make the book look more relaxed but I find them quite helpful to locate a certain item like helpful tips or a word of caution. I am certainly not the first one to use them so I am sure you know how they work!

The icons I am using were purchased (yes, *paid for*) from ☻ ImageEnvision.com. They have a huge variety of all kinds of clip art.

I decided to name the red dude "Nutty", deal with it ;). ☞ Table 1 shows the key to what the different icons (Nutty's different appearances) will be used for.

Table 1: Icons and graphics used in this guide.

	Nutty as a professor will point to a reference that might come in handy like a table with shortcuts for instance.
	What this poor fellow is carrying is a big question. This indicates a section where I try to answer the most commonly encountered questions. FAQ if you wish.
	What happened here??? When you see the test tube with Nutty spilling out a word of caution will follow.
	Nutty will try to explain a somewhat more complicated procedure or chain of events so follow carefully.
	When Nutty holds a light bulb it signals an idea. Why not try this for a change?
	The newest achievement of the Microsoft Office package: the Office Button. When you see this it means you have to click on the button.
	The well-known Windows XP start button; below is the Windows 7 equivalent. When you see this, click on the one in your Windows task bar

Screenshots

Let's be honest: humans (at least we males) are rather visual creatures… Keeping this in mind I tried to use illustrations, e.g. screenshots, wherever I thought they might help understand a certain task or locate a certain item on the screen (or even printout). Sometimes they will also show a result to give you an idea of what the procedures should have produced.

Cross-References

There it is: the first term that I will describe in much detail later on! Basically, a cross-reference points to another location in the same document, very similar to a hyperlink. Depending on the Word settings the mouse pointer will change to a hand (🖑) either immediately when hovering over a cross-reference or when pressing ctrl simultaneously (check your settings → Word Options → Use ctrl+Click to follow hyperlink). When following this link you will jump for example to a different section, a graphic or table. Cross-references are very useful and they will be explained in more detail ☞ later. *Note: In this document I tried to add a hand symbol ☞ everywhere I refer to another place in the book since it is not always obvious where clickable links are. For external links (e.g. websites) I used the globe symbol 🌐 instead. The hyperlinks will (obviously) only work in the eBook version which can be downloaded at a discounted price from our website.*

Where to Start?

What Do I Need to Write My Thesis?

It is understandable that the writing process has to start *sometime*. The reasons may vary – Either time is running out, your supervisor(s) continuously bug(s) you, or you simply feel like you should start out of free will. The following sections will briefly outline what is necessary, what is optional, and what is plain nice.

Essentials

Well, this guide is definitely a good start! But wait – there is more! To make sure that everything will go smooth a few things should be prepared (not necessarily all at once but it will help to *know* what might be necessary throughout the writing process). Items listed in ☞ Table 2 have proven very helpful for me, not only when writing scientific papers but also in general when working long hours on the PC. All items will not apply to everyone but hey, we're all individuals ;), and change is the spice of life!

Before the Writing Process

Computer Recommendations (Software)

Antivirus software. Sigh. The old scourge of the Windows world: Trojans, viruses, worms and other parasites trying to destroy someone's life. Meh. I have used different free or commercial packages and currently I am very pleased with Kaspersky Internet Security.

Word processor. I use Microsoft Word included in the Microsoft Office 2007 Professional Edition. The Professional Edition might be a bit overkill for some folks and if you would like to see which suite suits you best, take a look at the official 🌐 Microsoft Office website.

Table 2: Check list for a successful start!

ITEM	check
Backup CDs/DVDs, Flash drive etc.	☐
Coffee/tea/favorite beverage	☐
Comfy chair	☐
Computer that runs stable (!!!)	☐
Highly recommended: 2 screens!	☐
Image viewer/editor/scan software	☐
Instant messenger for emergencies	☐
Internet connection	☐
Microsoft Office 2007	☐
Music	☐
Notepad	☐
Patience	☐
PDF converter	☐
Pens, pencils, highlighter, eraser etc.	☐
Printer	☐
Printing paper (cheap for drafts)	☐
Scanner	☐
Snacks for those seemingly endless sessions	☐
Telephone	☐
Understanding partner	☐

Spreadsheets. Again, I used the Microsoft Office 2007 Professional Edition that, just like every other Office 2007 version, contains Excel. The new version is very powerful and has very pleasant visual features. However, the option of filling bars in graphs with patterns is no longer included (although old charts will still be displayed properly) because of the unlimited number of colors to choose from. Unfortunately, this is pretty bad for scientific documents since many publishers prefer black and white graphics over fancy, multi-colored charts. In addition, printing (and publishing) in color is usually more expensive. But don't worry! There is a free tool out there that can fill this gap!

The followings specs were taken directly from the Microsoft website:

Table 3: Microsoft's recommended specifications for Office 2007.

Computer and processor	500 megahertz (MHz) processor or higher.
Memory	256 megabyte (MB) RAM or higher. 512 MB RAM or higher recommended for Instant Search.
Hard disk	1.5 gigabyte (GB); a portion of this disk space will be freed after installation if the original download package is removed from the hard drive
Drive	CD-ROM or DVD drive
Display	1024x768 or higher resolution monitor
Operating system	Microsoft Windows(R) XP with Service Pack (SP) 2, Windows Server(R) 2003 with SP1, or later operating system.
Other	Connectivity to Microsoft Exchange Server 2000 or later is required for certain advanced functionality in Outlook 2007. Connectivity to Microsoft Windows Server 2003 with SP1 or later running Microsoft Windows SharePoint Services is required for certain advanced collaboration functionality. Microsoft Office SharePoint Server 2007 is required for certain advanced functionality. PowerPoint Slide Library requires Office SharePoint Server 2007. Microsoft Internet Explorer 6.0 or later, 32 bit browser only. Internet functionality requires Internet access (fees may apply). * Instant Search requires Microsoft Windows Desktop Search 3.0.
Additional	Actual requirements and product functionality may vary based on your system configuration and operating system. For complete requirements visit http://www.microsoft.com/office/products

PDF converter. There we are. Decisions, decisions! There are a lot of free and commercial tools out there that will make a PDF document out of your Excel, Word or virtually any other files. For now just one word of caution: Many of them will be working as a ☞ printer and might not support all functions in Word like bookmarks, hyperlinks, or comments. I used Adobe Acrobat Professional (but Standard works just as fine). Microsoft actually offers a plug-in for PDF export free to download here (http://www.microsoft.com/downloads/details.aspx?FamilyID=f1fc413c-6d89-4f15-991b-63b07ba5f2e5&displaylang=en) in case it was not included in your installation.

 Don't be scared by the enormous price tags of commercial software packages! Many companies now offer a fully functional trial version (Microsoft has a 60-day trial version for their Office suites). There are lots of online merchants out there like amazon.com that sell licenses for a fraction of what Microsoft, Adobe, or local stores ask for. Especially as a student you are entitled to some sweet deals!

Instant messenger (IM). IMs are not only for chatting between bored teenagers but also offer a very good and quick (hence *instant* messenger) way to get help from friends. I don't even keep track of new programs; I used mainly Skype, ICQ, and Yahoo, although lately I am exclusively on Skype. If you have questions, several ways to get in touch with me can be found on the ☞ Contact page.

Computer Recommendations (Hardware)

PC. One doesn't need a high-end gaming machine to write a thesis (although it is fun to have). I am not going to recommend a certain processor or graphics card since they change too quickly anyway. Instead, I will share my experience with different systems. There are just a few things that I can recommend:

- Have enough **RAM** to quench Windows XP's memory thirst. It has become very affordable. However, XP (32 bit) will only "see" 3 GB so unless you are intending to run a 64-bit system (XP, Vista, or Windows 7) more than 3 GB is unnecessary. Give 🌐 eBay or 🌐 amazon.com a try!

- **Video card**, well, I can't hold it back. I have enjoyed the luxury of owning a multi-screen graphics card for a number of years. There is nothing better than having your raw data or results on one screen and your Word document on the other. Or the internet browser. Or a video. Or this book.

- **Removable media.** CD/DVD burner and USB flash drives are essential. Not only for backing up data but also for transferring files from one computer to another, e.g. the lab to your home PC. Everyone knows that, hence, just a friendly reminder.

Periphery. The choice of peripherals really depends on how much you want to do at home with regards to printing, scanning, etc. and how much you can and *want* to invest.

- **Monitor.** I find that a monitor is the most important connection between you and your PC. It should be easy on the eye, 19" or larger, or even two if the budget allows (see Video card above).

- I have my own **printer/scanner** which actually sucks as a printer (it takes 2+ minutes for a color page). However, the scanner part is pretty decent.

- One thing that seems to drive everyone else except me nuts is my ergonomic **keyboard** (Microsoft Natural keyboard 4000). I have been using it for so long, at home and at work that I couldn't live without it. My bunnies and my clumsiness are responsible for my buying at least one new keyboard each year. Bummer.

- **Mouse**. I prefer wireless mice not only because my bunnies see the cables as a snack but also because of the freedom they offer. I have been very happy with my 🌐 Logitech MX Revolution but I also loved my (wired, R.I.P.) 🌐 Razer Copperhead. When going wireless make sure to have a stack of backup batteries or get a mouse with a docking station with built-in charger.

General Recommendations

- **Most importantly**, make sure to **back up your data regularly**! There is a backup software built into Windows XP; you might just have to install it separately (⚙ how-to). Google is your friend to find other freeware programs that will do a better job. Ideally, you have an additional physical device to store your backup files on such as a portable hard disk or USB flash drive. I have become used to partitioning my hard disks into at least two partitions: one for the operating system (OS) and program installations and another one for my own data. That way, if you have to reinstall the OS you can format the C: drive without touching the personal files. Obviously, you will still have to re-install all the programs and, most likely, reconfigure them! *Note: Many programs will save their configurations to the C: drive independent of the My Documents location. You might want to locate all important files before erasing data on the C: drive. Also, in case of a hardware failure, both partitions can be affected since it is the same hard disk!*

- When you start editing your thesis file(s) you should develop the habit of saving it under a new file name. For example, add the current date to your file name. This way, you will have different versions (or revisions) that you can access in case you are unhappy with your changes or the newest version is lost or corrupted. There should be no excuse not to have an external hard disk for backups since storage has become very affordable.

- Have Word save **AutoRecovery** information regularly (☞ Figure 1):

  → Word Options → Save → Save AutoRecovery information every xx minutes.

Figure 1: Set AutoRecovery options. For larger documents saving will take some time so you have to weigh safety vs. speed. You can also define the file locations here.

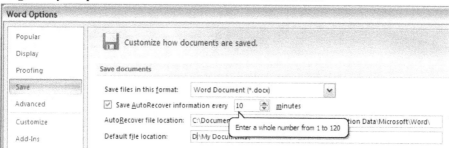

- To make your system run more efficiently defragment the hard disk regularly. Windows-freebie "Disk Defragmenter" (Win XP/7: 🟢 *start* / 🌐 → All Programs → Accessories → System Tools, unless you have moved the shortcut) is pretty basic so I would look out to find other solutions. I have been using ⊕ PerfectDisk for several years now and never had any trouble. There are a 30-day free trial and various versions available.

- **Take breaks**. I highly recommend that you get away from your PC every now and then. Not only will you get an opportunity to stretch and get some fresh air but also clear your mind. Coming back after the break might let you spot some mistakes or flaws that you overlooked earlier because you were so entangled in your work.

Planning Your Project

Guidelines

Official Guidelines

There are most certainly official guidelines issued by the college, university, or department that explicitly state the requirement for the thesis. So:

Before you start writing anything, check on your College/University/department's website what requirements your thesis has to fulfill. You should find information about the minimum and maximum page numbers, font-size and type, paragraph format, general structure (header/footer, page margins), information to be included etc. It would be a shame if you started compiling your document just to find out that you did it all wrong! On the other hand, if you follow this guide you will be able to change most of these properties very easily even after you started!

General Guidelines

Most commonly, scientific theses are structured like scientific publications:

- Abstract/Summary
- Introduction
- Materials and Methods
- Results
- Discussion
- List of abbreviations
- Acknowledgements
- References

The order might vary slightly, either determined by the institution or the preference of the writer.

Working With Multiple Documents

When I wrote my PhD thesis I used Office 2003. In the old Word version there was an option to have a Master document and several subdocuments. This allowed having a set of small documents that are connected via the Master document, thus, saving separate smaller files instead of a single large one. The way to do this might have changed but it is still true that the earlier you begin with thinking about the structure of your thesis the easier the process will be! You could, for example, have separate documents for the introduction, materials and method, and results. If you are interested, please continue reading this chapter or skip to ☞ Office 2007 Design.

Please DO NOT create separate files for different chapters of your thesis unless you intend to combine them in a Master document. The problems you will encounter are numerous:

- *Formatting will be different unless styles match exactly*
- *Table of content will not work properly unless the same styles are used*
- *Cross-reference will most likely not work*
- *Page numbers might get messed up*

However, if you follow the guidance in this and other chapters you will find a way to work things out.

The Outline View

I bet that most Word users never touched this feature. Understandably so since there is not much to see unless you know what you can do. Check it out: go to the View tab in the Ribbon and click on the Outline icon in the Document Views group. The appearance of your document changed drastically but there is no need to worry as long as you don't mess around with options in the new Outlining tab (☞ Figure 2) that appeared in the Ribbon.

Figure 2: The Outlining tab is visible only when Outline view is selected.

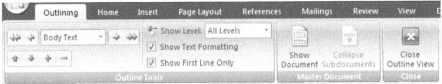

The Outline view will demonstrate how important the correct use of ☞ styles is. In this viewing mode any style that is formatted as a heading (e.g. Heading 1) will be displayed together with the associated paragraph, shown as bullet points. This way it is very easy to follow the structure of the document with regards to formatting; a good document should not only read well but the content should be supported by the formatting to group content by a solid structure.

Creating a Master Document and Subdocuments

Before I tell you how great a Master and subdocuments can be a word of caution that has been widely discussed in the online world: Master documents are prone to becoming corrupted due to the complex nature of a Word document. Some experts even recommend to not use this feature at all: http://word.mvps.org/faqs/general/ WhyMasterDocsCorrupt.htm)! It worked great for me but you have been warned!

If you are serious about splitting your thesis into Master and subdocuments let's get started! First of all you should have a good folder structure for all your documents. I have seen people go crazy and have one folder for each section. I usually have one folder for each type of document that I will need, such as Word files, Excel workbooks, and pictures. *I highly recommend having a backup folder on a separate hard disk so that your work can be restored in case the main storage or even just individual files get corrupted.* However you decide to do it, do it early on!

Next, I would like to suggest reading up on ☞ templates and ☞ styles. Although Word has been improved in the way it handles styles it is better to be on the safe side and use the same template containing exactly the same formatting instructions for all the subdocuments that you might create. So please take the time to familiarize yourself with these sections and come back.

Welcome back! Now that you know how you can create and manage styles and use that information to create a fantastic template that is tailored for your thesis needs we can start with the Master document. Create a new file from your thesis template. Switch to Outline view as shown ☞ above. Click on the Show Document button to reveal the Master document options (☞ Figure 3). Now you have the tools that you need to create, insert, and manipulate subdocuments.

Figure 3: The Master Document options let you create, insert, and manipulate subdocuments.

Before you can go crazy with your subdocuments you should start by outlining your document. You can start with the very basic headings similar to the suggestions in the ☞ General Guidelines above. Just for fun I changed them slightly as shown in ☞ Figure 4. Initially you will only see the grey circle with the "-" inside. The text you type next to it will be formatted as a heading with the specified level. Every time you press Enter you will create a new heading of the same level. To change the level, i.e. to define subsection headlines, press the tab key to indent the headings (not shown).

Figure 4: The first step in structuring the thesis is to define the headings. You can define multiple layers of structure by indenting the headings to become subsection headings (not shown).

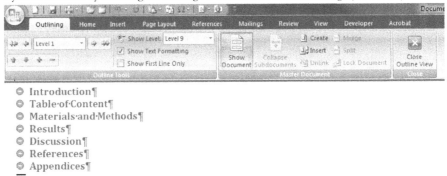

To create a subdocument place the cursor in one of the headings and click on the Create button in the Master Document group. I used the Introduction as an example. After you clicked on the Create button a bullet point appeared underneath the heading and a box formed around the heading and the bullet point (☞ Figure 5). The text that you enter next to the bullet point will be treated as a separate document if you so desire. To open the section as a new document that can be saved individually double-click on the document icon top left of the grey circle with the "+" inside. As long as the subdocument is linked to the Master document changes made in either will be saved and visible in both files.

Figure 5: The first subdocument has been created! The text with the bullet point can be opened and saved as a separate document which is linked to the Master document.

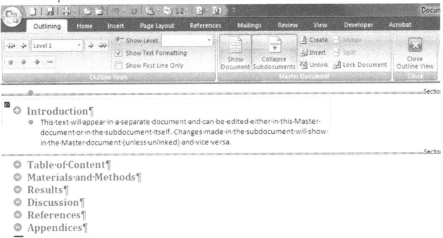

In case you already have a document that you want to insert in your Master document position the cursor where you want the text/content to appear and click the Insert button.

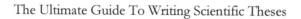
If you want to separate a subdocument from its Master document but keep the content in the Master document click on the Unlink button.

I can only emphasize that you should pay attention to the styles that your documents are using. If you have only text to copy insert it and keep the destination formatting. If not take the time and format the text using your Master document styles.

You have now mastered (pun intended) the art of creating a Master document and as many subdocuments as you like. If you want to continue with separate files or create one big document is really up to you – just another decision for you to make.

Office 2007 Design

Installation

To take advantage of all the benefits that the Microsoft Office Suite offers special attention needs to be paid during the installation process. After entering the license key you will be taken to the installation screen where you can choose from several options, including the installation path and the features to be installed:

Figure 6: Installation options for Microsoft Professional 2007. Many goodies are hidden in the tree structure so don't forget to browse through the options!

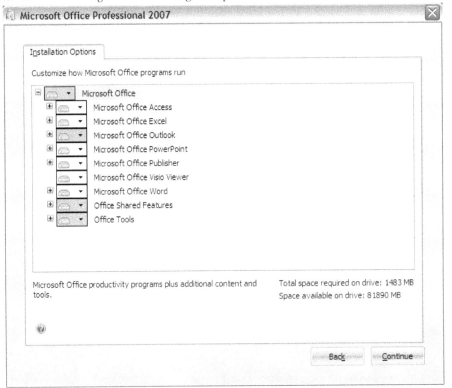

 Please take the time to browse through the options of each program (click on the ⊞ signs to expand the selection; you might find interesting and helpful features like additional import and export filters, more templates, clipart, and so on. On the other hand, you can also disable all the unwanted features and programs.

Where Are the Menus?

Once you have gone through the installation process, you will be greeted by a completely different user interface than what you are used to. Oh wait, upon the first program start you will be asked to activate the product; just another way to ensure that you are using a legal copy of Microsoft Office. Anyway, the new design is the biggest change from previous Microsoft Office versions: the old fashioned menus have been replaced by the "Ribbon"; that's what the bar at the upper part of the window has been named.

Apparently, the Microsoft Support Team realized that many people have been confused by the completely new design of the good old Office programs. So they came up with tutorials that aim at helping users of older Office versions find commands in the 2007 design. These tutorials can be found here:

🜚 *Tutorial for Word* | 🜚 *Tutorial for Excel* | 🜚 *Tutorial for PowerPoint*

The best way to get accustomed to the new design is just to look around and try out what you find (or check out the tutorials mentioned above). You will notice that the content of the Ribbon will change depending on what you select in the main document. For instance, a Picture Tools - Format tab will appear when a graphic is selected. Tables have even more options. There are also lots of guides and handbooks out there that will deal with the new design. Visit my 🜚 website for updated content.

The developers did not include one of the tabs in the Ribbon that is essential when designing forms and interactive elements: The "Developer" tab. To activate it, you have to go to the Options:

 → Word Options → Popular → Show Developer tab in the Ribbon

Customizing the Quick Access Toolbar

The mighty Quick Access Toolbar is small and poorly populated when any Office program is run "Out-of-the-Box". It looks somewhat like that (☞ Figure 7):

Figure 7: Pathetic version of the Quick Access Toolbar – Make it grow!

Three icons are displayed, one for **Save**, **Undo**, and **Redo**. That's it. The first thing you might want to do is to customize this powerful little helper. There are several ways to achieve that:

1. → Word Options → Customize;
2. Click on the small arrowhead, pointing downwards, on the toolbar and select **More Commands…**;
3. Right-click anywhere on the toolbar and select **Customize the Quick Access Toolbar…**

All three options will lead you to the following screen (☞ Figure 8):

Figure 8: The screen that shows you how flexible and powerful the Quick Access Toolbar really is. Cryptic but still helpful information will pop up when you hover with your mouse pointer over a command.

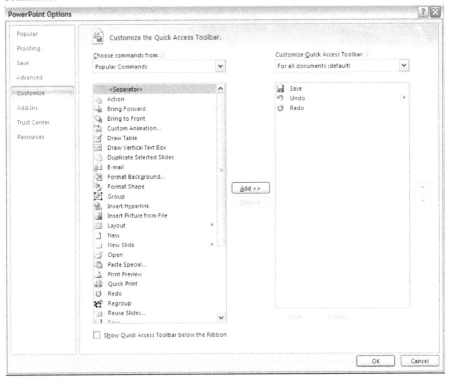

To add an item (command) from the left selection panel to the right (which represents the Quick Access Toolbar) you can either double-click on the item or select it and click the "**Add >>**" button. The selection will appear either at the very end of the right panel or *underneath* the last selection there. The up and down arrowhead buttons let you change the order. If you cannot find what you are looking for select **All Commands** from the upper left drop-down menu. Selecting a "**<Separator>**" will add a vertical line in between the icons. It is even possible to change the Quick Access Toolbar for each document! Simply change

For all documents (default) in the upper right drop-down menu to the name of the file you want to associate the Toolbar with.

Now that you know how to add, move and delete icons why not give it a try and customize the Quick Access Toolbar? You'll see later on that this might save you precious time! This is how my Quick Access Toolbar looked like at some point while I was writing this document (☞ Figure 9):

Figure 9: Sometimes size _does_ matter and will provide a much more useful Quick Access Toolbar.
My favorite commands include Close, Open, Print, and Insert Symbol.

Copying the painstakingly customized Quick Access Toolbar from one PC to another (or for backup purposes) is not as trivial as it sounds. While the actual customization files _are easily located in_ `C:\Documents and Settings\[username]\Local Settings\ Application Data\Microsoft\Office` _(Windows XP) or_ `C:\Users\ [username]\AppData\Local\Microsoft\Office` _(Windows Vista or Windows 7), the_ transfer _requires some preparation. Because I am not the author of these steps and they are very nicely documented on the Windows TechNet website, here just the link:_

🌐 _http://support.microsoft.com/kb/958062_

Once this is done you can copy the customized `.qat` _file into the correct directory and_ voilà – _the Quick Access Toolbar looks like you expect._ Note: _Each Office 2007 program comes with its own_ `.qat` _file. Outlook 2007 even has multiple files!_

I am convinced that you will change the Toolbar throughout the writing process to adapt it to your writing style as you discover which functions you use the most.

More useful Options

There are a lot of useful functions hidden in the Word Options. They let you change how many operations that are usually run in the background, will perform. Obviously, I will only mention those that I deem important or helpful.

Forgotten Goodies: Document Properties

How often have you received a document that you thought might serve you well as a template for your own creation? Or even when you create a document from scratch and just fill the pages with content… you are missing out on some really useful features of each Word document.

Just like a good web page Word documents can have metadata that are not directly visible because they are not part of the page content. They are saved with the document as *properties* though. You can define a number of document properties that can (and will) be used by search engines or whose content can be referenced/displayed interactively in the document.

To see what properties can be stored in a Word document, go to Options → Prepare → Properties. You will notice that an information bar has appeared above the document. It contains only a few fields: Author, Title, Subject, Keywords, Category, Status, Comments, and Location (read-only). These are also the most important properties of a regular Word document to be honest. If you want to see *all* available options click on Documents Properties ▼ next to the information symbol and select Advanced Properties... The information on the first tab is actually very close to what you would see in older Word versions when you select "Document Properties" from the file menu. Besides the properties mentioned above you can customize several variables which is presumably unnecessary for a thesis.

Adding tags to your document (via document properties) will help you organize your files by category, status, keywords, identify you as the author, and so on. Additionally, once the information is stored in the tag it can be inserted into the actual Word document (e.g. as ☞ cross-reference) and will be updated automatically. Keeping the meta data updated is also a very good way to avoid creating a document that states someone else as the author when another Word file was used as template.

Note: To be on the safe side, always update all fields before printing or converting a Word document into a PDF. This will be done for example when you select 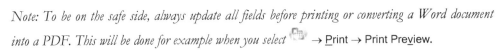 *→ Print → Print Preview.*

AutoCorrect and Proofing

To make life, well, setting up documents easier, Word offers a variety of tools. Opening the Proofing Options will open a screen as shown in ☞ Figure 10.

Figure 10: Word 2007's proofing options. Here you can find a lot of automated little helpers for correcting and formatting your text automatically.

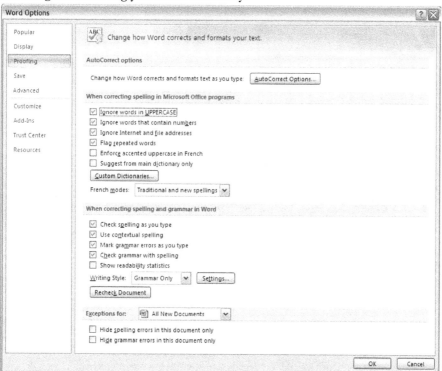

Clicking on the AutoCorrection Options... button will bring you to another world of possibilities. ☞ Figure 11 shows an overlay of three tabs in the AutoCorrect menu. Adjusting the settings to your preference might be very helpful. Not only can you change a lot of features that you might find annoying, for instance that Word automatically starts a new list when you type an asterisk at the beginning of a new line. You can also add sequences of text that will be converted automatically into symbols of your choice. Some of the options are redundant in the sub-sections which definitely shows that the programmers tried to make the menus more intuitive!

Figure 11: Some of the most important features for AutoCorrect. You can tell Word whether to insert lists automatically, change ordinals to subscript, substituting a sequence of characters with a symbol and much more.

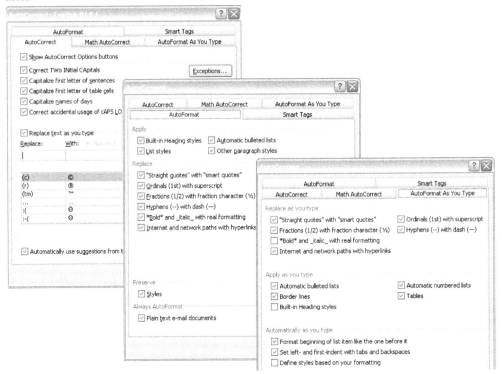

Here are some automatic corrections that I usually change or add:

- Instead of the default arrows in the Wingdings font (←,→,↑,↓) with the more elegant version found in the Symbol font (←,→,↑,↓)
- Usually two capital letters at the beginning of a word are changed to only the first letter being capitalized. For scientists for example that can be annoying when you type DNase or RNase. There is an Exceptions… button (tab **AutoCorrect**) where you can specify which words should not be changed. Alternatively, once you typed the word that you don't want to be changed again, move the cursor inside the word where a small white-blue bar will appear under the first letter. Once you move the cursor over that bar a lightning symbol with a drop-down menu will pop up in which you can select Stop **A**utomatically Correcting "xx".
- You might want to consider removing the (C) to © AutoCorrect. A manual way around it though is to write (C[space])[space] then move the cursor back and remove the space after the C. Another manual way is to press the backspace key right after the AutoCorrect function did its job. This will undo the AutoCorrect action.

- Consider adding long words that you always use and that should not be abbreviated to the list of automatically replaced text.

Miscellaneous

Just a couple of more things: you can change the color scheme of the Office programs by clicking → Word Options → Popular → Color Scheme (☞ Figure 12).

Figure 12: Word (Office) 2007 color theme options. The selection isn't huge but at least you don't have to stick with the standard blue.

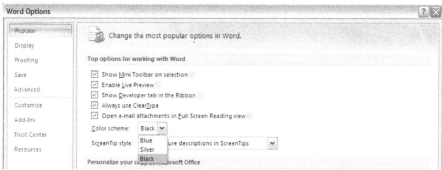

Please note: This will affect all Office programs that support this feature so you won't be able to have a blue Word, a black Excel, and a silver PowerPoint!

If you are mainly writing on one set of documents like your thesis you might find it helpful to set the default file location to the folder where you store your project:

→ Word Options → Advanced → File Locations (at the end of the screen)

By default, Word 2007 saves its files in the new `.docx` *format. Since not all people have the new Office suite it might be necessary to convert the file to the old-fashioned (and actually bigger in size)* `.doc` *format. To save an existing document in a different format:*

→ Save As ▸ will show you the most common options.

In case you want to change the default format for Word 2007 go to

→ Word Options → Save → Save files in this format *and select the format that you fancy the most. It is highly recommended to use the* Word 97-2003 document *version* `.doc` *when you know that your collaborators do not have the latest Office version.*

Again, if you are nosy just browse around and try some of the features or check out other guides to get a better picture.

Using Microsoft Word

Elements of a Word Document

This is where I start talking about the actual use of Microsoft Word. Word has a ton of really useful features such as Themes, ☞ Styles and ☞ Templates, ready-to-use and included for free. Additionally, a lot more can be downloaded directly from Microsoft or elsewhere in the WWW. But first let's start with the basic definitions of a page in a Word document.

Page Size, Margins, Orientation

If you look at ☞ Figure 13 you will see the page specifications can be altered in the Page Layout tab. There is virtually no limit to the [reasonable] page size. Orientation can be changed between landscape and portrait. Page margins define the space that will not be used by regular text in the document. The top and bottom margins are used for the header and footer, respectively, while the left and right margins are usually empty since many printers have "unprintable" areas right there. Also, when writing a thesis margins will be needed for the reviewers' comments and of course for the binding. It is possible, if not highly likely, that the institutional requirements will advise on the margins. As mentioned above, to use different page sizes and orientations in one document ☞ sections have to be defined.

Figure 13: Page specifications.

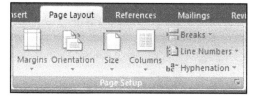

One question that always appears is how to insert one landscape page whilst keeping all others in portrait. ☞ FAQ 1 will give answers!

Page and Section Breaks

Everyone knows what a page is: it's the (most of the time white) rectangle that you see on the screen and on which you place content of your document, i.e. your text and other objects. A page is defined by the page size, orientation, and margins. You can add a watermark, headers and footers, page numbers, have text displayed in more than one column and so on. But what about sections?

Page Breaks

Honestly, when I receive documents that are poorly formatted it *annoys* me. One of the biggest nuisances is when the author continuously hit the Return key until the next page is reached (although in very rare instances this is necessary). There is an easier and most of all more flexible and elegant way: position the cursor in front of the text you want to have on a new page and press ctrl+Enter. Instead of carrying around all the useless empty paragraphs (because that is what pressing the Return key does) there will be a clean cut and the text behind the Page Break will *always* appear on top of a new page.

Unless you have enabled **Show Formatting** *(ctrl+* on the keyboard or click the ¶ button in the* **Home** *tab) you will only see that the text behind the cursor moved to the next page. Enabling the option will show a dotted double line with* **Page Break** *written in the middle.*

Sections

Well, actually most of the features mentioned above are specifications of sections rather than pages. Think of a page as the physical entity that has content. On a page you have at least one section. In each section you can define the page size, orientation, number of columns, different headers/footers etc. You will find references to sections a lot, trust me.

If you want to know more about how Word handles everything behind the curtain check out the VBA help! There you will find the following hierarchy:

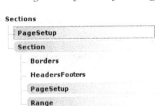

Not sure what section you are currently in? Right-click on the **Status Bar** *at the bottom of the Word window and check* **Section** *to immediately see the information and select it to display it in the* **Status Bar***.*

Section Breaks. Do you still remember what I wrote about sections? The power of sections is reflected in part by the number of options you have to insert a section break. To see what flavors they come in, go to the **Page Layout** tab of the ribbon (☞ Figure 13).

When you click on Breaks ▼ the section menu will appear (☞ Figure 14):

Figure 14: Options for Section Breaks.

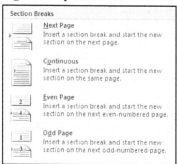

What the different Section Breaks do is pretty much explained in the menu. The two first options (**Next Page** and **Continuous**) will be used most frequently since a thesis is usually single-sided and does not need different even and odd pages. But before you get to confused let's just do it, shall we?

1. Open a New document (ctrl+N or [icon] → **New** → Blank Document)
2. Open "nonsense.txt" (included in the bonus archive)
3. Copy the entire text (ctrl+A, then ctrl+C)
4. Switch to the new, blank document
5. Paste the text (ctrl+V)
6. Click somewhere in the middle of the text, then go to the Page Layout tab of the ribbon
7. Click on Breaks and select Section Break → Next Page
8. To explore the opportunities you just unlocked go back to the Page Layout tab and play around with the different options like Orientation or Size (see also below). You will see that only the section that the cursor is in will change. I will talk about more specific applications later on so don't be scared!

FAQ 1 – How To Insert A Single Landscape Page

Let's say you want to add an extensive table or a wide image/chart that does not fit on a regular portrait-oriented page. There are two ways to do that:

1. Type some random text and select it either with the ☞ mouse or using ☞ keyboard shortcuts. Go to the Page Layout tab and click on Margins → Custom Margins… (or click on the Dialogue box launcher). This will open the Page Layout dialog box (☞ Figure 15).

   Figure 15: Part of the Layout dialog; an easy way to insert a page with a different orientation.

   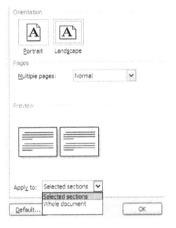

   Select Landscape in Orientation and Selected sections or Selected text in Apply to. Click OK.

2. You can also manually do what Word was doing in the first option: insert two section breaks, one before the new landscape page, the other one after. Move the cursor to the end of the page after which you want to have a landscape page. Go to the Page Layout tab then Breaks and select Section Break → Next Page. Repeat the step. Move the cursor to the page you just inserted and click on Orientation → Landscape in the Page Layout tab.

To see what happened press ctrl+* unless formatting symbols are already shown.

Headers and Footers

The correct use of headers and footers can make a huge difference on the appearance and usability of a document. You should *at least* include the page numbers and your thesis title somewhere on each page. Creating one set of header and footer for the entire document is very simple. Word offers predefined layouts that are available with one click. Switch to the Insert tab of the Ribbon and you will find a Header & Footer group (☞ Figure 16). When you click on any of the buttons a drop-down list will open that shows available predefined header and footer designs. Page numbers can be positioned anywhere in the margins and come in different flavors as well.

Figure 16: The Header & Footer group offers easy formatting of the header and footer.

Another, much quicker way, to insert your custom header or footer is to double-click either in the header or footer area and start typing. This will grey out the main document and open a new tab in the Ribbon with options to format headers and footers (☞ Figure 17) that includes the Header & Footer group from ☞ Figure 16.

Figure 17: The Design tab for headers and footers appears when editing either one.

 You will see me repeat this several times. It is important to understand that headers and footers are properties of sections and not the page or document. By default a new section's header and footer are linked to the previous section so they are apparently the same. However, you can have different headers and footers for each section. See ☞ FAQ 2.

Double-check your page numbers if you decide to have multiple sections. Sometimes when you unlink footers or headers the page numbering starts at 1 again. To remedy this open the header/footer and highlight the page number. Now click on the Page Number ▾ *button in the* Headers & Footers *group of the* Design *tab. Select* Format Page Numbers... *and make the necessary changes (e.g. check the* Continue from previous section*).*

Headers and footers can be defined differently for odd and even pages or the first page since this is a very common requirement. Click on the Dialog box launcher [icon] of the Page Setup group (Page Layout tab). The Page Setup dialog will open (☞ Figure 18). Select the Layout tab and you will see a Headers and footers group. For example, you decide to print two pages on one sheet (duplex) and want to display the page numbers always on the outside of the page, select Different odd and even. Most likely you want to have a cover page without page number so select Different first page as well. Make sure you select where you want to apply the changes (Apply to drop-down); your options are Whole document or This point forward. Your layout will be displayed schematically in the Preview group.

Figure 18: The Page Setup dialog not only lets you change the paper size and margins but also the layout for headers and footers.

FAQ 2 – Customize Headers and Footers

 If you want to include more dynamic information in the header or footer than the page number you will have to work extensively with ☞ section breaks. Each time you want to change the header or footer you have to define a new section. This is very closely related to ☞ FAQ 1 – How To Insert A Single Landscape Page; but instead of changing the page layout we define different headers and footers. You should familiarize yourself with the two section breaks that you might be using: A break on the next page and the continuous break. The first option creates the new section on the following page and creates a page break whereas the latter will also create a new section starting with the following page, however, there will be no page break. Let's get busy!

1. Open the file "Headers_footers.docx", provided in the bonus archive.
2. Place the cursor at the end of the first paragraph and go to the Page Layout tab then Breaks and select Section Break → Next Page.
3. On the new page double-click in the header section and uncheck the Link to Previous option.
4. Delete all text and insert a ☞ cross-reference to the Heading text of the second heading (check ☞ FAQ 8 – How To Insert a Cross-Reference).
5. Close the header (either click the button or double-click in the main document).
6. Now place your cursor at the end of the second paragraph and go to the Page Layout tab then Breaks and select Section Break → Continuous.
7. Go to the next page and repeat step 3.
8. Delete all text and insert a cross-reference to the Heading text of the third heading.
9. Close the header.

Here's what you did: you created two new sections with different headers. Each header will display the text of the heading. Inserting a continuous section break is very useful when you don't want a page break before your heading but still change the header on the next page. A tutorial video can be found on my website (🌐 academia-nutcrackers.com/videos).

If you inserted dynamic content (e.g. a cross-reference to heading text) into the header make sure to go into ☞ Print Preview to update the fields!

Content of a Page

Now that we have talked a little bit about the appearance of a page we should take a look at how to fill a page with content. The more you take care of structuring the content logically the easier it will be throughout the writing process. A very simple example: Let's say you decided on Times New Roman size 11 as the default (or Normal) font and formatted your headings as a bold, size 14 font. It might happen that the institutional guidelines require the headings to be underlined. Without telling word that headings are headings and not "normal" text you will have to go and change each and every heading manually to reflect your new style (I will explain ☞ later what a style is; it has nothing to do with wearing the latest fashion since I would be no help there at all ;)). That said – here are the most important structural contents of a page.

Headings

Headings should be short and descriptive of the subsequent text. Only when the heading is interesting and appropriate you will catch the reader's attention and make him/her want to read more. Headings are usually formatted such that the reader can scan the document and find the content of interest more easily. They will also appear in a table of contents and are linked to the next paragraph in order to keep the heading with the following text. Hence, make sure to give headings their own style (see ☞ below). You should also think about a hierarchy of headings early on. For instance, think if you want Roman numbers (I, II, …) for the first heading, then 1, 2, … for the next level and so on. If you need some ideas go to the Home tab and click on the Multilevel List button . Check out ☞ FAQ 3 for a quick way to structure your headings properly. If you don't like the pre-defined format read the ☞ section on formatting to get helpful hints to change it!

Paragraphs

Paragraphs contain big chunks of text/information or maybe just a few words. The point is that paragraphs usually span more than just one or two lines in a document. Logically, they should contain pieces of information that somehow belong together. Spacing between paragraphs and other elements like the next paragraph or the headings should be chosen carefully for a good design. You will find ☞ tips on formatting further down in this book. Make sure to conform to your institutional policies when formatting a paragraph with font size, line spacing, indents etc.

Numberings, Bullets, and Lists

I briefly touched on that in the ☞ Headings section above. We all know what lists are and for a while now, Word has automatically converted lines of text starting with a "–" or a

"*" into a bulleted list and into a numbered list if you start your paragraph with a number and a dot (like "1."). Formatting lists as such is not only very easy and results in a consistent design but also enables Word to refer to these items internally (☞ Table of Contents).

 Sometimes you will need more than mere numbers in your list. For example, you are writing a step-by-step guide and you want to have the word "step" in front of the numbers. No problem! Word lets you add text anywhere around the numbers. Click on the down arrow head next to the numbering button *. Select "*Define New Number Format...*". In the* **Number format** *box you can add text anywhere next to the number which is shaded in gray (Figure 19). A preview is given in the dialog as well.*

Figure 19: Options for the definition of a new numbering format.

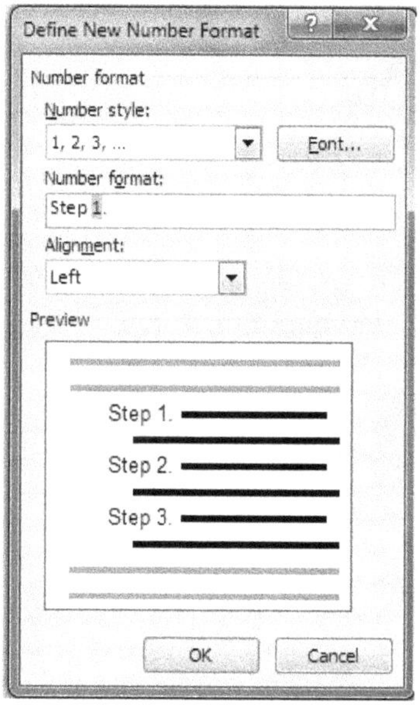

Lists have different levels that reflect some kind of hierarchy. For bulleted lists that will be different bullets (symbols) for numbered lists you can choose between a variety of options. You can even define your own bullets in case the standard symbols are not satisfying; it helps to have lots of fonts installed. If you want to play around with different lists and how they look like, they are located in the **Home** tab in the **Paragraph** group as . As a very important example, the hierarchy of ☞ headings is discussed in FAQ 3. Alternatively, try a table to design your very own list. How? Check out ☞ FAQ 4!

FAQ 3 – Structure Your Headings With A Multilevel List

A good thesis starts with a solid structure. The best way to achieve a solid structure is to define styles for each of the headings and associate a numbering system. This numbering system reflects the hierarchy for each heading level. Word 2007 offers a potent solution: Multilevel lists. Admittedly, they are not that easy and can be a pain but if you follow this FAQ you'll get your document structured in no time!

1. Open the file called TOC.docx which is provided in the bonus archive.
2. Place the cursor in the first heading ("Main Heading 1") and select the Multilevel list button from the Home tab in the ribbon.
3. To make it easy select the 6th pre-defined list, i.e. row 2, column 3, in the menu that opens. Here is what happened with just one click:
   a. You defined a multilevel list with regular numbers (1, 2, 3 etc.)
   b. Every new level is numbered including the previous level numbers (e.g. 2.1, 3.1.1 etc.)
   c. Every level has been linked to a ☞ Style (in this case Heading 1, Heading 2 etc.)
   Note: If you would like to learn how to do this step by step yourself, please visit 🌐 *www.academia-nutcrackers.com/videos for a tutorial video.*
4. To assign the new multilevel list, i.e. the structure of your headings, to the actual heading text simply click on the desired Heading QuickStyle in the Styles group of the Home tab in the Ribbon.

Since you now have a solid structure in your Word document you can use this structure to populate a ☞ Table of Contents very easily.

Tables

A very convenient way to collect and display data is to use tables. But tables can also be used for design purposes (like in most web pages nowadays): without visible gridlines elements can be positioned and grouped fairly nicely.

Word 2007 has a decent repertoire of ways to design a table. So let's get started creating one! First, switch to the Insert tab and click on the only icon in the Tables group. The appearing pop-up lets you select how many rows and columns the table shall have. Whilst selecting the range of the table Word will insert a preview at the cursor position. Once you are happy with the basic structure click the left mouse button. Word will insert the table and switch the ribbon to a new tab named Table Tools - Design. There you will be confronted with several suggestions how to make your table more appealing. Here are some features located in the Table Tools - Design tab → Table Style Options that might save you a lot of time:

- *Header Row.* The first row of the table is different and can be formatted independently.
- *First Column.* The first column of the table is different and can be formatted independently.
- *Banded rows/Banded Columns.* Basically, odd and even rows/columns have different formats, e.g. shading and borders.

To adjust the effect of these options on the table click on ⬚ in the **Table Styles** group. You can either modify an existing style (<u>M</u>odify Table Style...; careful! you will overwrite the style if you save it) or design your own (<u>N</u>ew Table Style...). Make sure to select only that part of the table which you actually want to modify – there are a lot of options as shown in ☞ Figure 20. As you can see, your creativity will not be limited!

Figure 20: Very helpful formatting options for tables in Word 2007.

Talking about creativity… In Word 2007 you can even *draw* your table! Just like using a pencil! To get started, select the **Insert** tab and click on the (only) icon in the **Tables** group. From the drop-down list select <u>D</u>raw Table and go crazy! First you have to define the outer border/frame of the table. After that you can add columns and rows to your liking. *Tip*: You can also use a very similar feature in an existing table to format the borders of an existing table. Click somewhere in a table, in the **Table Tools - Design** tab of the Ribbon, a **Table Borders** Group will show up. When you click on the **Draw Table** icon you can draw table borders with the format selected left to the icon.

 You will definitely benefit from using a Table Style if you want to use one or more of the following formatting options:

- *Alternate formatting of even and odd rows or columns, including borders, shading, even text formats*
- *Different border at the end of the table*
- *Consistently formatted tables throughout the document*
- *One-click formatting of a table*

If you ever tried to keep up manually formatting a table so that the last row has a solid border while the others have none or a different style, or distinguish rows visually by using 2 different colors… you know the pain of manual table designs!

FAQ 4 – Table With Automatic Numbering

Have you ever tried to write a step-by-step guide using a table? Your first question might be: Why would I want to do that? Don't I have the convenient **Numbering** and **Multilevel List** buttons in the Ribbon? One click and I have a numbered list! Well, separating the numbering structure from the body text lets you format both entities independent of each other. A numbered table also allows you to insert graphics and other objects which is almost impossible to do in a regular list.

If you enter the numbers manually and want to insert a row you will have to change all the numbers after that. One way to avoid this problem is to create a table in which the first column (assuming that this one will contain the numbers) is formatted as a ☞ numbered list.

1. First, create a table containing 5 rows and 3 columns.
2. Resize the first column to 1".
3. Move the mouse pointer just above the first cell of the first column; it will change to a thick arrow pointing down ⬇.
4. Left-click to select the first column.
5. Click on the numbering icon in **Home** tab, **Paragraph** group. This will insert numbers in every cell.
6. If you don't want the dot behind the number move the cursor to one of the numbers and click on the down arrow head next to the numbering button . Select "**D**efine New Number Format…". Change or delete the dot in the **Number f**o**rmat** box. You can also create more elaborate multilevel lists as described ☞ earlier.
7. Adjust the tabulators as required (☞ Tabulator (Tab) Stops).

The result can be found in "numbered_table.docx" in the bonus archive. Every time you insert a row it will automatically number each row accordingly. You can, of course, change the indentation of the numbering also; after all it is a regular paragraph. *Note*: You will not be able to define a multilevel list if you don't enter text behind the numbering. When you leave an item in a list empty and press return Word 2007 will automatically remove the list format at this position (for numbers and bullets) or decrease the level (multilevel lists).

TIP: to insert a new row at the end of the table go to the last cell and press the tab *key* ⟻.

I won't go more into detail of what else you can do with tables. That would surely be beyond the scope of this book.

Images, Graphics, Objects & Co.

Inserting images, graphics, and other objects can drive people nuts! For some reason Word *never* seems to do what the user wants when it comes to placing objects in a document. And this is quite true: a computer never does what the user wants but what the user *tells* it to do! When inserting an object other than placing it in line with the text, either the object moves randomly across the page or the text looks funky; the depression, aggression, and frustration factor is very high. This is most frequently happening just because the user does not *know how Word actually handles* the positioning of the object.

In this section I will try to elucidate what happens when you insert an object and what you can do to prevent Word from messing up your document. For a quick start go directly to ☞ FAQ 5.

1. It is not only highly recommended but necessary for this step to show formatting symbols *(ctrl+* on the keyboard or click the ¶ button in the Home tab)*.
2. First, open the document called "Graphics.docx" included in the bonus archive.
3. Click somewhere in the first paragraph to place the cursor inside the text.
4. Select Picture from the Illustrations group in the Insert tab. A window will open where you can select which graphic to insert. I included a random graphic ("insert_graphic.gif") in the bonus archive that you can use but feel free to insert whatever you like.

5. If you have not changed the default setting for inserting pictures (→ Word Options → Advanced → Insert/paste picture as:) it will appear at the position of the cursor in line with the text.
6. Let's play around with the options you have now. Select the image and click on the Text Wrapping icon (Arrange group) in the Picture Tools - Format tab:
   a. *In line with text*. Just as the name suggests; this will place the image in line with the text

   b. *Square*. The image will be surrounded by a rectangular box around which the text "flows".

c.   *Tight*. If the image you inserted has a non-rectangular shape, for example a GIF file transparent background or a vector graphic like WMF, the text will flow around the outline of the image.

d.   *Behind/In front of Text*. These options place the image on its own layer either behind or on top of the text without any wrapping.

e.   *Top and Bottom*. No text will be left or right around the object.

f.   *Through*. Almost the same as Tight with the difference that text will also flow inside the graphic wherever no outline is. *Note*: I haven't yet seen that effect independent of the image I inserted.

g.   *Edit Wrap Points*. Very neat feature. Shows you the actual frame that is used as a "border" for the object. You can modify it to your liking.

h.   *More Layout Options…* Opens a dialog window with even more details. And this is where we will find the solution to most problems! Check out ☞ FAQ 5 – Make Objects And Text Play Together Nicely.

FAQ 5 – Make Objects And Text Play Together Nicely

We all know the frustration: You insert a graphic or Excel chart into your text and as soon as you edit your document the objects seem to have a life of their own. The key to prevent this from happening is to understand how Word deals with these objects and how they are "connected" to the text.

The Anchor

If you tried out the tutorial above that showed you the different ways to wrap text around a graphic you are somewhat familiar of what Word can do. Have you noticed the anchor symbol ⚓ that appears on the left side next to the paragraph start as soon as the image is no longer in-line with the text? This symbol indeed fulfills the function of an anchor as it connects the object to the text. As soon as you move an object the anchor will move as well and adhere to the beginning of the closest paragraph. Try it by dragging a graphic across the document and watch the ⚓ jump from paragraph to paragraph. If the text (paragraph) moves to a new page the anchored graphic will also move. The most common reason for documents getting messed up lies in the involuntary incorrect use of the anchor. What happens frequently is that the object is either anchored to the wrong paragraph or the anchor is moved when the object is moved. Additionally, *deleting the paragraph that the object is anchored to will also delete the object.* To put an end to most of this go to the advanced layout options (an object must be selected):

Picture Tools - Format → Text Wrapping (Arrange group) → More Layout Options... or right-click on the graphic then select Text Wrapping ▸ → More Layout Options...

Figure 21:The Advanced Layout dialog - where most of your graphic troubles end!

Check the Lock anchor check box and confirm with OK. You will see that the anchor symbol has changed to ⚓. Whenever the object is now moved it will always be attached to the paragraph it was locked to. *However, once locked the object cannot be moved to a different page than the paragraph it's anchored to.*

This trick will work for every object that has an anchor, even captions (when they are inside a text box).

Captions

Having fancy pictures and impressive charts is important for every thesis. Even if a picture speaks more than a thousand words some explanatory text has to accompany the image or chart. Word offers captions for exactly that task. Captions are more than just plain text for descriptive purposes. They come with their own style (see ☞ Styles below), can be ☞ cross-referenced and be used to create a ☞ Table of Figures.

To insert a caption select the item you want to add the caption to, select the Reference tab from the ribbon and then click on the Insert Caption button. A dialog window will open (☞ Figure 22, shown with optional dialogs) in which you can choose the options for the caption.

Figure 22: The Caption dialog. The main window (center) will let you choose the label and where to place it. A new label can be defined as well as the numbering style (left). The AutoCaption option lets you select for which object Word will automatically insert a caption (right).

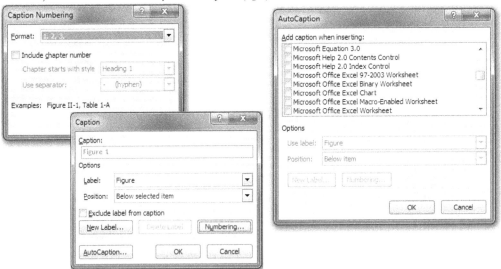

Whenever a caption is added you can either pick a previously defined label from the drop-down menu shown in ☞ Figure 22 (center) or click on the New Label... button to define a new label. Word will automatically add the next highest number to the label and you can start adding text in the Caption: text box; you will be able to add or change that text and its formatting after you close the dialog. Next, choose the position where the caption will be placed: Either above or below the selected item (check with the institutional guidelines if there are preferences).

FAQ 6 – Adding Text (Captions) To Figures, Tables, etc.

Usually captions are used for labeling tables, figures, or equations. These three options are readily available when you insert a caption:

References tab → Captions group → Insert Caption

Besides adding your own caption text (<u>N</u>ew Label…), e.g. `Fig.` instead of `figure`, you can also decide how the numbering should look like (☞ Figure 23). Or if you know that every time you add a certain object you want to have a caption to go along you can enable the <u>A</u>utoCaption… feature. Don't be scared by the menu that pops up there; it is just a selection of all the different (OLE) Objects that you can possibly insert. If that's too much, I recommend inserting captures manually. It always worked for me so far!

Figure 23: Insert a caption. You can modify the label identifier, numbering, and enable automatic captions.

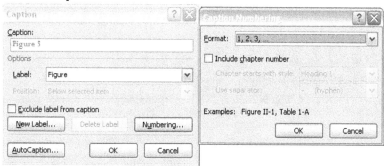

Although figures and other objects in a thesis are usually numbered consecutively, you can decide to include the chapter number (☞ Figure 23).

There are numerous benefits of having Word number figures, tables and such. For example moving objects with their captions will automatically add the correct number (or to be more precise: the number will be updated to reflect the changes). I added a short section on how to add a caption in ☞ FAQ 6.

Don't forget to make a cross-reference to the inserted object by linking to its caption. It is very confusing and also bad style to have pictures, tables, charts, etc. showing up with no apparent relation to the surrounding text. The same is true for the opposite: whenever you insert an object you should also add a caption to briefly describe what you are showing.

Benefits of adding a caption *using the built-in function are numerous:*

1. *Captions come with their own style so if you have to change the appearance (e.g. increase/decrease font size, make it bold) it's done by changing the* ☞ *style;*

2. *Labels will help you to keep track of each item that you defined a label for, e.g. a figure, table etc.;*

3. *When you move the item and its caption the numbers will reflect the new position if it changed;*

4. *The caption will always be with the item that it was defined for assuming it is* ☞ *in line with the text. This is achieved because Word automatically enables the "Keep with next" formatting for the previous paragraph for captions below the item or for the caption itself if it was placed above the item. For items not in line with text Word automatically creates a text box around the caption.*

5. *Captions can be cross-referenced to very easily;*

6. *You can very easily insert a* ☞ *Table of Figures;*

Caption text and Table of Figures.

One word of caution: If you intend to insert a Table of Figures (TOF) please be aware that the entire caption text *will be included in the TOF (just like in this book). This is very often undesirable because figure captions (legends) should contain a description of the figure or even some background information about how the figure was obtained (e.g. experimental details). On the other hand, a short information in the TOF like "Figure 5: Western blot results of knocked-down gene product." can be very helpful. See* "Generic mouse study.docx" *(bonus archive) for an example.*

The initially somewhat tedious work-around requires that you are familiar with how to ☞ *create and modify Styles:*

1. *Modify the Caption style: set the* after *spacing to 0 pt and make sure to check the* Keep with next *option; this will prevent separation of the first and second part of the caption.*

2. *Create a new style based on the existing Caption style; this way, the new style will change whenever the original Caption style is changed. Name the new Style* Caption 2.

3. *Check that the* before *spacing of the paragraph is set to 0 pt and that the* Keep with next *option is enabled. Save the new style. Note: You can change more properties of the new style, e.g. the main caption (what appears in the TOF) should be bold but the following text not.*

4. *Modify the Caption style again: set the* Style for following paragraph *to* Caption 2. *Save.*

5. *When you now add a caption, press* Return *after you added the text that is supposed to be included in the TOF.*

6. *Type some words in the new paragraph (which should now be in Caption 2 style and not appear in the TOF).*

Copy and Paste for Pros

Have you ever thought about what is actually happening when you do the good old "copy&paste"? Windows has a nice feature that is called the Clipboard. Microsoft's developers seem to have a thing for naming virtual features after their real-world counterparts. The Clipboard collects and holds information that can be retrieved when necessary. You will probably only know one layer of the Clipboard – the last object you put in.

If you want to see how the Clipboard works select the **Home** *tab in the Ribbon and click on the Dialog box launcher* 🔲 *in the* **Clipboard** *group. A new task pane will open on the left edge of the screen. If nothing has been copied into the Clipboard yet this space will be empty. However, if you already used the* ctrl+C *function the objects will be listed there, text as text and thumbnails of images when possible. As soon as the mouse pointer hovers over an item in the Clipboard list a down-arrowhead will appear. Clicking on it will let you either paste the object (just like clicking on the item itself) or delete it from the Clipboard. Just try it! Open the Clipboard task pane, select different objects, an image, some text, maybe a table, and copy them using* ctrl+C *and see how the list gets populated! Using the* ctrl+V *command will only paste the last, i.e. topmost item in the list. It is basically like a real pile of papers – last in, first out.*

When you copy and paste an object from one application into another, let's say from Excel into Word, using either the keyboard short cuts ctrl+C then ctrl+V Word will decide how and in which format the Clipboard content will be inserted. Sometimes, if not most of the times, that is not exactly what you had in mind.

Simple Copy and Paste

So let's analyze what happens when you have an Excel chart that you want to place in your thesis. Open an Excel workbook that contains a chart. Click somewhere on the chart to select it and press ctrl+C. After you switched back to Word, place the cursor where you want the chart to appear then press ctrl+V to insert it. I can almost guarantee you that the result is not what you wished for! The text in the chart title and legends is out of scale, everything is shifted etc. You did not only insert the chart but merely opened a connection between Word and Excel, also known as *embedding*. The great advantage of this connection is that every change you make in the Excel chart is reflected in the Word document. The obvious downside is that you don't necessarily get in Word what you saw in Excel! And this works both ways: You can modify the inserted chart to satisfy your needs inside the Word document but its appearance in the source [Excel] file is now (most likely) messed up.

Whenever you need to embed an object into another application, e.g. Excel into Word, remember that modifying it will result in changes in both *the source file and the target application. If you want to keep the original Excel file but also want to be able to independently modify the chart in a Word document you should create a copy of the file and work with that. Obviously, if you change data in the original Excel file you will have to make these changes in the copy as well!*

If you don't care about changing the inserted object, meaning that you have a final version, there are multiple ways to make it look the way you want it to. Even if you go back to the original document and make changes – another copy&paste is just a few clicks away! See ☞ FAQ 7 for more details.

More Sophisticated Ways to Paste

It happens that you don't necessarily want to get out of the Clipboard what you have put in it. Sounds confusing? Here an example: Assume you have an Excel table that you want to paste into a Word document. Simple `ctrl+C` followed by `ctrl+V` will insert an editable Word table. Word might change the layout of the table to adjust to currently used styles. Resizing the table will also result in text shifting and line breaks (instead of just making the table plus its contents smaller). If you don't care about editing the table and you want to preserve the overall appearance you should consider inserting it as a picture instead of the automatic HTML format. Now you might be wondering "what can or should I paste then?". That, of course, depends on what you want to achieve and also what options you will be given, depending on the source of your object. Some ideas are listed in ☞ FAQ 7.

Now that we know *how* we can insert objects and place them correctly why not look at the options *what* we can insert? Sometimes the choice is easy: If you want to insert an existing JPG file you can simply drag&drop the file into the position in the document where you want it to appear. Or you can go to the Insert tab in the Ribbon and click on Picture. But sometimes you have to make the decision *how* you want to paste it. In this FAQ I will explain the most commonly used formats and elaborate why certain objects should be inserted this way or the other.

Bitmaps (BMP, TIF, PCX, JPG, GIF, PNG, etc.)

Bitmaps are composed of individual pixels. Each pixel has color information, thus, the more pixels and the higher the maximal number of colors (bits) is, the bigger the picture is. Compressed formats like JPG have an algorithm that reduces the file size significantly with the downside of losing quality. TIF, BMP, or PCX in contrast are lossless but big. GIF pictures are limited to 8-bit grayscale or 8-bit color and can have a defined transparent color or region. PNG is a fairly recent format that allows more colors than GIF and still offers transparency options.

As a rule of thumb, if you need sharp, crisp edges or transparency in a bitmap, go for GIF or PNG. If you want to insert a large, colorful, and solid graphic then choose JPG to reduce the image size.

Vector graphics (EMF, WMF, CMX, etc.)

For those who are somewhat familiar with advanced math will recognize the term "Vector". It is a mathematical object that lets you display lines based on coordinates and other information. In contrast to bitmaps, not each pixel is stored but rather the equation for the line or object like a rectangle or square. The advantage of vector graphics is that they can be scaled up and down without loss of quality. However, due to the nature of vector graphics, images with a lot of detail like photos will not transform well. Some of you might know online applications that transform a photo into a cartoon; well, that's about what will happen if you export a bitmap into a vector format – it becomes scalable but loses a lot of detail. The following objects are perfect for being inserted as a vector image (*If the pasted format is different from the original the object cannot be edited with the original application!*):

- Excel and other charts, incl. Flowcharts
- Tables, e.g. Excel sheets
- PowerPoint graphics
- Text (as long as you don't need to edit it).

References

Everyone has experienced that documents will become confusing and unmanageable the longer they get. So far I have mentioned how a page looks like (☞Page Size, Margins, Orientation) and what elements it can contain (☞Content of a Page). The next step is now to make use of References to link to other places in the document. Word 2007 has dedicated an entire tab in the Ribbon for this purpose. It contains six groups: Table of Contents, Footnotes, Citations & Bibliography, Captions, Index, and Table of Authorities. Because I am convinced that a well-structured thesis (or Word document in general) *needs* a decent internal reference structure, I will elaborate on some of the options in the Reference tab.

Table of Contents

The most essential reference in a document is the Table of Contents or short TOC. Although Word has had the option for an automated TOC for a very long time now, few people use it. Instead, they screen the document once it is finished and type in the headings and page numbers manually. Bad idea! Just a few changes in the document can result in the TOC being null and void.

Word has a very nice way to avoid the hassle of inserting page numbers manually. However, the user has to follow a couple of rules to make it work smoothly:

1. Every heading that you want to appear in the TOC needs to be formatted properly. *Note: this formatting does not reflect how the reference in the actual TOC will appear; these are separate styles!* For each level of the headings (technically it is a multilevel list) the user has to define separate ☞ Styles that will be linked to each level in the multilevel list (☞ Numberings, Bullets, and Lists). Read FAQ 3 – Structure Your Headings With A Multilevel List for suggestions.

2. Each heading has to be formatted using the style that was linked to the multilevel list. An easy method is to save the style in the ☞ Quick Style menu and simply click on it to instantly format the heading.

Sounds easy enough, doesn't it? Now that the way is paved for a nice TOC all that's left to do is select the References tab in the Ribbon and click on the Table of Contents ▾ button. A list with pre-formatted TOCs will appear but for our purpose we will select Insert Table of Contents... to be able to completely customize it! You will be greeted by a dialog like shown in ☞ Figure 24:

Figure 24: Table of Contents dialog window. The actual appearance will differ based on the styles used in the document.

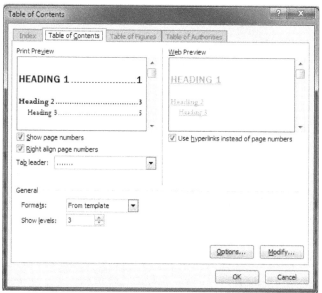

So far that doesn't seem very exciting… In this dialog you can change whether page numbers shall appear in the TOC (I haven't found a reason why they *shouldn't!*), how the space between the heading caption and the page number will be filled (empty, with dots, etc.), how many levels of the headings will be included in the TOC and a few more options. However, when you click on the Options… button another small but very important dialog will appear (☞ Figure 25). Now you will realize why it is so important to structure the headings properly: Each level of the TOC can be associated with a separate style. That means that everything that has been formatted using these styles will be included in the TOC so be careful how you use them – e.g. use a "Heading 1" style only for headings that you want to appear in the TOC. You can manually assign TOC levels to each heading. That allows you to reflect the hierarchy of your multilevel list in the TOC as well.

Figure 25: The Table of Contents Options dialog. In this dialog you can associate styles with levels of the TOC. Everything formatted with the selected styles will be included in the TOC.

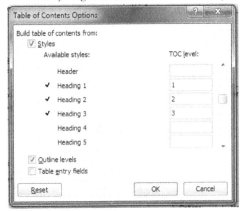

 A Table of Contents (TOC) is technically nothing else but a field and fields are in general not updated automatically! So it will happen that when you add headings to your document they will not appear in the TOC immediately. Instead, you have to either click somewhere inside of the TOC and press F9 *(which is the shortcut to update fields) or select the* References *tab in the Ribbon and click on the* Update Table *button. Alternatively, go to* → Print → Print Preview.

To change the appearance of the TOC you have to modify the ☞ Styles named TOC*n* where *n* is a number from 1-9 or "Heading". Each number reflects a different level within the TOC. You can format each level individually and "have it your way".

Table of Figures

No surprises here – a Table of Figures (TOF) neatly summarizes all the figures in the current document. It works like a TOC; instead of headings, however, it uses the ☞ captions of figures to populate the list. Although the name sounds restrictive to figures, you can in fact have a TOF for any label that you defined for captions.

You will find the button to insert a TOF in the References tab of the Ribbon. A dialog similar to ☞ Figure 26 will appear with a variety of options to choose from. Here you can select which label you want to create a table for (select from the drop-down menu next to Caption label), if there should be any Tab leaders and how the TOF will look like in general.

Figure 26: Dialog for inserting a Table of Figures. A TOF is essentially a TOC for figures or other objects with a caption. The appearance can be changed easily: Either choose from predefined Formats or create your own style (Modify…). Note that the text of the caption will also be displayed.

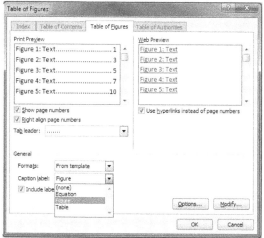

 Be careful when you select to automatically insert a Table of Figures (TOF). As shown in ☞ *Figure 26, the TOF will include the* text *of the caption as well as the label if included. That means if you are used to write elaborate captions (which is great!) be prepared for an unpleasant surprise. Fortunately, there is an "easy" way around that was discussed in the* ☞ captions *section above.*

Footnotes and Endnotes

I have never really needed to implement footnotes or endnotes so I will keep this short. If you want to add an explanation to your main text but don't want to put it in the main text then footnotes is what you are looking for. There are two different options where the explanations will appear: footnotes and endnotes. A footnote means that the text will appear at the bottom of the current page (or right below the text if selected) whereas an endnote will place the text at the end of the document (or end of the section if selected).

In the Ribbon, go to the References tab and click on the Insert Footnote button. A screen like depicted in ☞ Figure 27 will pop up. Depending on your selection of Insert Footnote or Insert Endnote, the other selection will be grayed out but you can always convert one into the other. You assign numbers or symbols to your foot/endnotes, either across the entire document or just for the current section (see ☞ Sections).

Figure 27: Footnote and Endnote dialog window.

Citations & Bibliography

Another option of Word that I, admittedly, have never used myself. Whenever I needed citations, I used the program 🌍 Endnote which is available separately, and is usually provided (or something similar) at the institution that you write your thesis at. Because of my lack of experience I can only refer to the Microsoft Online help:

- 🌍 General overview of new features
- 🌍 Create a bibliography

Some of this content can also be found in the Word help, i.e. through the integrated Online help. Maybe I will have more to say in the next edition…

Cross-References

Now we're talking! This section will be very helpful and might keep you from running into stupid and time consuming mistakes. I highly advise to read the section on ☞ captions before continuing here. Before we can get started let's define what cross-references are and then check what we can refer *to*!

What are cross-references? A very simple example: You have a figure somewhere in your document. As a good student you want to mention it in a paragraph, or *cross-reference* it. A cross-reference can also function as a hyperlink so that when you click on it you will be taken to the referenced object (this is enabled by default but can be turned off). The beauty of this is that if you move the figure (and the caption) everything will automatically be updated in the cross-reference. Depending on the object that you want to refer to this could be the page number it is on, the content of the object and so on.

Differences between cross-reference and hyperlink

Initially, I never really thought about the difference. Both seem so similar! A cross-reference can be inserted as a hyperlink ("link"), meaning that if you hold the `ctrl` *key and click on the link the cursor will move to the position that the link refers to. But honestly, that's about all of the similarities! Below is a table of what cross-references and hyperlinks can and cannot do (☞ Table 4). You will find both methods have been used extensively throughout this book.*

Table 4: Comparison of cross-references and hyperlinks. This table gives an overview of what a cross-reference and a hyperlink can be used for. The reference text is the part of the text will be used for the reference and function as hyperlink if selected.

Task	*Cross-reference*	*Hyperlink*
Use text as hyperlink to jump to a different position in document	✓	✓
Freely choose text to use as hyperlink	✗	✓
Link to other documents, files, or online resources	✗	✓
Link to bookmarks and other defined places within the document	✓	✓
Use caption as reference text	✓	✗
Automatically update the reference text used as hyperlink, for example when a headline that is referred to changes (in other words refer to text and display that text as hyperlink)	✓	✗
Display page number as reference text	✓	✗
Display relative position (above/below) as reference text	✓	✗
Display paragraph numbers as reference text	✓	✗

A couple of examples:

1. *Cross-references are very useful for an overview list like "the study was divided into three sections:" followed by cross-references to the heading (check* **paragraph text** *of the heading or numbered item) of each of the sections.*

2. *A hyperlink is really only useful when you want to use your own text to point to another place in the document or if you want to link to other files or resources. For example, you have a heading for a section about SDS-PAGE. Instead of using the heading text for cross-reference you can create a hyperlink using "how to run an SDS-PAGE" as text.*

What can I cross-reference? As mentioned just a second ago, all objects (more accurately their captions) can be cross-referenced. This includes pictures, tables, equations, diagrams, charts – you name it! But the list goes on; when you go to the Reference tab of the Ribbon and click on the Cross-reference button a dialog like shown in ☞ Figure 28 will appear. The list under Reference type is pre-populated with numerous items such as Numbered item, Heading, Bookmark etc. Whenever you define a new ☞ caption label the label text will be added to this list. I will explain the meaning of the default items right here:

- *Numbered item*: Whenever you start a ☞ numbering list you can refer to any one item.
- *Heading*: If you have been listening to my advice and structured your document by ☞ defining headlines you can refer to them here.
- *Bookmark*: Bookmarks are like their classic counterparts; you mark a spot in your text and assign it a unique identifier. Pretty much like an anchor in HTML. If you ☞ set any bookmarks, refer to them here.
- *Footnote/Endnote*: Make sure you don't lose track of where you inserted ☞ footnotes or endnotes.
- *Equation*: Refer to a Microsoft Equation object.
- *Table* (not visible in ☞ Figure 28): Refer to ☞ tables via their captions here.

The drop-down menu Insert reference to: will be described below in ☞ FAQ 8.

Figure 28: The cross-reference dialog. First, select the reference type which will populate the large space which is shown empty, with available items. Next, specify what you want to refer to (Insert reference to); sometimes there are multiple options.

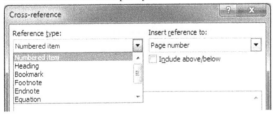

How do I insert a cross-reference? ☞ Figure 28 shows your main tool for inserting a cross-reference. A drop-down menu offers you a variety of options to choose from. In Word you can*not* create a *cross-reference* to an inserted object *directly*. However, you can create a cross-reference to the ☞ *caption of the object*; just another reason to thoroughly label your objects properly!

One possibility is to simply type "Figure 2 shows…". It's quick and apparently works great (until you move, add or delete figures and all your hard-typing is out of order). Fortunately, there is a better way.

Bookmarks

Bookmarks in Word 2007 are closely related to the real-world equivalents: you can place a bookmark virtually anywhere in the document and use a ☞ cross-reference or hyperlink to quickly jump to its position. It is very useful if you want to be able to refer to a position within the document without having to format it in a special way since a bookmark does not show in, or in any way change, the appearance of the text. You can insert either a cross-reference to the text that was marked as bookmark, the page number, relative position (above, below) or simply create a hyperlink using text of your choice.

FAQ 8 – How To Insert a Cross-Reference

One tip up front: You should consider adding the cross-reference button *to your Quick Access Toolbar. Follow the ☞ few simple steps described in the beginning of this book.*

☞ Figure 28 shows the dialog that opens when you select Cross-reference *from the* Captions *group in the* References *tab. As mentioned in the text above ☞ Figure 28, first select the item (type) that you want to cross-reference from the* Reference type *drop-down list. Depending on the selection the drop-down list labeled* Insert reference to: *will change. Below is a summary of the options that you will be given with a brief explanation.*

Insert reference to option	Available in reference types	explanation
Above/below	*All*	*Inserts the word above or below depending on the position of the referenced object*
Page number	*All*	*Inserts the page number of the referenced object*
Paragraph number (no context or full context)	*Numbered item; Bookmark*	*Inserts the value of the number of the list item; all text that is included in the numbering will also be shown: I have not seen any effect for bookmarks yet*
Heading number (no context or full context)	*Heading*	*Inserts the value of the number of the list item of text formatted as heading; all text that is included in the numbering will also be shown*
Paragraph text	*Numbered item*	*Inserts the text behind the numbering value, e.g. if the numbered item is 1. Open a document it will insert "Open a document"*
Heading text	*Heading*	*Inserts the text behind the numbering value of the heading, e.g. if the numbered item is 1. Introduction it will insert "Introduction"*
Bookmark text	*Bookmark*	*Inserts the text that has been selected as bookmark*
Footnote/Endnote (also formatted)	*Footnote; Endnote*	*Inserts the number or symbol of the end- or footnote; if the formatted option is selected it will be displayed just like the end- or footnote, e.g. superscript*
Entire Caption	*Equation; Figure; Table; custom labels*	*Inserts the entire text that is included in the caption of the respective object.*
Only label and number	*Equation; Figure; Table; custom labels*	*Inserts only the label and sequential number, e.g. Figure 1*
Only caption text	*Equation; Figure; Table; custom labels*	*Inserts the entire caption except the label and number*

As you can see, many of the available references overlap and give you great flexibility. This flexibility is one of the most important ☞ differences between hyperlinks and cross-references! Considering the

FAQ 8 – How To Insert a Cross-Reference

options you have to insert cross-references you have to choose which one is the most suitable. Here a few examples:

1. To refer to figures or tables select the appropriate type and then "Only label and number" from the Insert reference to: drop-down menu.

2. Use "Above/below" if you want to refer to something you mentioned earlier or that you are going to describe later.

3. I use "Heading text" for example when I want to compile a list of headings outside the Table of Contents. Very helpful to give an overview of steps in a protocol.

4. Similarly, the "Paragraph text" can be used to create a list for numbered items that are not formatted as heading.

5. When to insert a "Page number" should be self-explanatory ;)

Formatting Elements

Styles

Styles, when used correctly, are an essential component of a properly structured document. Styles define the way characters or paragraphs will be formatted and thus appear on the screen and hardcopy (print-out). This section will be pretty detailed because I can only emphasize that properly defined and applied styles will be worth the effort although initially it might seem too tedious.

There are three different kinds of styles

1. Character
2. Paragraph
3. Linked (paragraph and character) → default

The name gives it all away: a "Character" style will only affect the selected character(s) while a "Paragraph" style will be applied to the entire paragraph the cursor is in. A "Linked" style, now that's fancy! If one or more characters are selected it will only change the font attributes (like a "Character" style) but if no character is selected the entire paragraph that the cursor is in will be changed (like a "Paragraph" style).

Quick Styles. Every one of the ☞ Templates comes with a set of pre-defined styles whose appearances vary according to the theme that is used. The **Home** tab in the Ribbon harbors the **Styles** group (☞ Figure 29). The actual styles in the menu will most likely look different but don't worry.

Figure 29: The Styles Group in the Ribbon showing available QuickStyles. Change text or modify styles with a simple click!

To edit all the details of a QuickStyle, go to the **Home** tab in the Ribbon and right-click in the box of the style, located in the **Styles** group, you wish to edit, and select <u>Modify</u>.... Alternatively, first open a fly-out menu of all styles by clicking on 🖰 ("Dialog box launcher") in the lower right corner of the **Styles** group and then right-click on any of the styles and select <u>Modify</u>.... The upcoming dialog (☞ Figure 30) will let you modify virtually any detail of the style that you can imagine: numbering, paragraph (only "Linked" and "Paragraph" styles), font, color, border, even language and a shortcut and so on. It also gives you a preview of what your text will look like as well as a summary of the text attributes.

Figure 30: Dialog to modify a Style. The true power of this dialog is revealed only after clicking on the Format▾ button (menu shown left). A summary of the style properties are given right below the sample text.

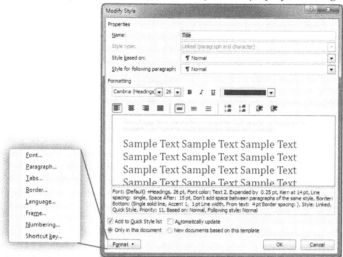

Let's analyze the dialog in more detail. First you should give your style a name. Be short but descriptive. The style type cannot be changed once a style has been defined so it will be grayed out unless you are creating a new style. The Style based on: drop-down menu lists all currently available styles that you can use as a basis to define your own new style. This also affects how the style will behave; for example, when creating a heading I highly recommend basing that style on an already existing heading style. That way you make sure it will appear in the list of Headings for ☞ cross-references. Basing a style on another one will result in changes when the base style is changed. For example, you create two additional headings (Heading two and Heading three) using Heading 1 as basis. When you change the font of Heading 1, Heading two and three will also be formatted using this font. An option that is very useful as I find is the next item: Style for following paragraph:. Obviously, this option is only available when the style is either a linked or paragraph type. The style that is selected here will be used for the next paragraph, i.e. after the Enter key is pressed. Hence, the selection in the drop-down menu only contains linked and paragraph-type styles.

The options to modify the appearance of the (selected) text or paragraph are sheer endless. I will not cover the details because everyone has their own taste! You should experiment on your own and find the best match for your purpose but keep in mind that there are most likely institutional limitations to what you can use for your thesis. The format options are discussed throughout this book.

There are four additional options that are not directly affecting how the style will look like but how it will be handled by the parent document. Uncheck Add to Quick Style list if you do not want the style to appear in the list shown in ☞ Figure 29. A word of caution about automatically updating the style is given below. Next, you can decide if you want the style only to appear in the current (active) document or if you also want the template (usually Normal.dot) to take over these changes.

While experimenting with a style it might be helpful to check the "Automatically Update" option. All changes that you make to the selected style in the actual document will be saved and the style will be updated. This is convenient as all changes are saved and applied immediately. But don't forget to turn it off when you are done because all instances of the style will change as well!

The menu shown in ☞ Figure 29 contains the Quick Style selections, styles that will be used most frequently and are available at the click of a button. A very neat feature is that you can preview the style before applying. By hovering the mouse pointer over the menu for one second or so the text around the cursor will change to reflect the selected QuickStyle.

The Quick Styles menu usually has several rows and you can either scroll through them by clicking 🔲 or 🔲 or expand the entire Quick Styles menu by clicking on 🔲. Latter action will also show you three additional menu selections: Save Selection as a New Quick Style, Clear Formatting, and Apply Styles. The first option comes in very handy when you just came up with a great looking format that you think you will use more often, for instance Greek symbols for alpha, beta, etc. This is actually a much better way than inserting a symbol.

Try it! Type "a", highlight the letter you just typed with the mouse or by pressing shift+← *and select "Symbol" from the font drop-down menu. The "a" looks like α now and should still be highlighted. Now click on 🔲 in the Quick Styles menu and select Save Selection as a New Quick Style. A dialog window will appear in which you can name the new Quick Style. Type "*Greek Symbol*" and hit OK. A new item appeared at the beginning of the Quick Styles menu.*

Templates

Templates are Word files that are used to create new Word documents. A template can already be filled with content like text, graphics, tables, forms, and such. It can also be apparently empty like the template "Normal" which is always used when a new, blank document is created (ctrl+N or 🔲 → New → Blank Document).

The difference between a template file and a regular Word document is, apart from the extension .dotx, that when you double-click on a template file in the Windows Explorer, a new document will be generated, based on the template. This does not change the content of the template file and can be very useful for data capture forms, reports, protocols, résumés, newsletters, or greeting cards. Consider it as making a copy of a document that you can work with and the original being safe in a different binder/folder. There are two ways to edit the template file: 1) Open it in Word like any other Word document (`ctrl+O` or 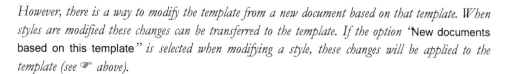 → Open) and 2) right-click on the file in the Windows Explorer and select "Open" from the menu.

However, there is a way to modify the template from a new document based on that template. When styles are modified these changes can be transferred to the template. If the option 'New documents based on this template*" is selected when modifying a style, these changes will be applied to the template (see ☞ above).*

Creating a Template

There is virtually no difference between creating a regular Word document and setting up a new template. You can fill your document with any content that you like. You can even open a document that you think has everything you need and save it as a template.

I highly recommend creating a template file for your thesis. It should include the following elements:
- *Defined ☞ footer and header, e.g. containing the title of your thesis, maybe even chapter titles, and the page number*
- *All the ☞ styles that you want to use. Really take the time to experiment and be done with it by the time you save the template (although of course you can always make changes later)*

If you decide you created a new document structure that you will be able to use again and again (like a fax cover page) save it as a template file:

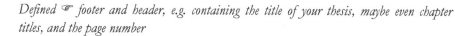 → Save As → Save as type: Word Template or

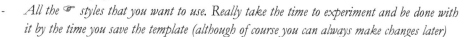 → Save As ▸ → Word Template

You will realize that the location to save the file automatically changed to the directory where Word templates are stored by default (see ☞ above on how to change that directory). *Note: If you are not sure that the new format can be read by everyone who needs the template, save it as Word 97-2003 compatible ".dot".*

If your template contains macros you will have to select Word Macro-Enabled Template *as file type or your macros will be lost. However, sometimes the Macros will still work when creating a new document that is still linked to the Macro-Enabled Template file. If anyone can explain to me why, please ☞ contact me!*

Using Existing Templates

If you want to experience the vast variety of already included templates go to → **New**. On the top left you have several options where to look for template files:

- **Blank and recent:** Shows the most recently used template files and the option to create a standard blank document based on Normal.dot
- **Installed Templates:** Lets you choose from a variety of templates for all kinds of occasions. You will have to be connected to the internet to enjoy the Microsoft Office online templates. You can also find user-generated and submitted template for example for writing a résumé that allows for direct submission to the Monster website.
- **My templates…:** Opens a dialog very similar to the one encountered in previous Word versions when creating a new document from a template other than Normal.dot. You will find templates that were saved in the default template folder (e.g. C:\Users\[User]\AppData\Roaming\ Microsoft\Templates).
- **New from existing…:** A file browser opens and you can select any Word-compatible document and create a new document based on it. This is very helpful when you have templates in different locations, e.g. all over the company/university network.

After selecting the template of your choice you will see that the document name changed to Document*n*, where *n* is a number that starts at 1 and increases by 1 for each new document. The next time you want to create a new document the last used templates will be listed in the recent document list.

Tabulator (Tab) Stops

Tab stops (or short "tabs") are another well underestimated and underused feature in Word. What do most people do when they want to align two lines of text? Either they press the space bar until it looks, well, "OK" or the more sophisticated Word users at least use the tab key (⭾). The latter method will at least make sure that the text is perfectly aligned, however, only the preset, left-aligned tab stops every half inch will be used.

All my tab stops

Tab stops are left-aligned, right? Or is there anything else? You bet! There is an unsuspicious square button (⌊L⌋) in the upper left corner just below the ribbon on top of the vertical ruler that changes between a number of states when clicked. If the ruler is not displayed the button will also not be visible. In this case, go to the **View** tab and check the **Ruler** check box.

Table 5: The tab stop selector and its hidden treasures. You can easily add tab stops or other indentation markers. * name as displayed in tool tip.

Icon	Name*	Details/function
L	Left tab	Text starts left of tab stop and moves to the right as you type (like normal, left-aligned text does).
⊥	Center tab	Text centers around the tab stop (like center-aligned text does in a paragraph).
⅃	Right tab	Text starts right of tab stop and moves to the left as you type (like right-aligned text does).
⊥	Decimal tab	Aligns numbers at their decimal point ("." or "," dependent on the national standard/language setting).
∣	Bar tab	Not for text positioning; instead, a paragraph-spanning, vertical line is inserted.
▽	First line indent	Sets the indent for the first line of text in a paragraph, i.e. all following lines might be indented differently (see Hanging indent below).
⌂	Hanging indent	Sets the indent for all but the first line of text in a paragraph, i.e. the first line might be indented differently (see First line indent above).

Inserting tab stops

☞ Table 5 gives an overview of the different kinds of tab stops that Word offers. From my experience I can say that these options more than suffice! There are two ways to take advantage of tab stops:

1. *The numeric way:* Double-click inside the horizontal ruler just below the Ribbon. The tab stops dialog (☞ Figure 31) should open. *Note: Sometimes the page layout dialog shows instead. Close it and try again.* You can enter the exact position of the tab stop and change the properties of all existing tabs. First, select the alignment (Left, Center, Right, Decimal, Bar; see ☞ Table 5 for explanations). Next enter the tab stop position. You don't have to use the English system; typing 5 mm will set the tab stop at exactly 5 mm but the number will be displayed in default units (e.g. 0.2"). Last but not least, click the Set button to create the tab stop. If you make a mistake you can either clear the selected tab(s) (Clear) or clear all tab stops at once (Clear All). You can also change existing tabs; select the tab from the list, make all necessary changes and hit the Set button. Here you can define the distance between default tab stops, i.e. where the cursor will move when the tab key is pressed but no other custom tab has been set.

Figure 31: The tab stops dialog. Use this dialog to define tabs based on exact numbers rather than the visual approach of dragging them inside the horizontal ruler.

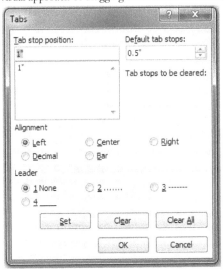

2. *The visual way*: A much quicker, and for some scenarios (e.g. ☞ FAQ 9) the best way is to select the type of tab stop by clicking on the tab stop selector and then click in the horizontal ruler at the position where the tab should appear. Once a tab is placed you can always drag it to another position; a vertical line will appear. You will see that it rather "jumps" than slides when you just click on the tab and hold the mouse button depressed while moving. Holding the Alt key during the movement allows for a smooth gliding.

Uses for tab stops

Now that we know the tab stop options, let's see what we can use them for.

1. Obviously, tabs should be used to *align text in different lines*. One example is a part of a document that needs a name and a date, e.g. for signatures. A nice way is to set a left tab such that date and name are aligned. A table could also be used but that is more time consuming.

2. Similar to item 1; e.g. a list of ingredients. You have the ingredient on the left side and want to have the amounts on the right, also right-aligned (☞ Figure 32A). A bit more sophisticated is the list in ☞ Figure 32B; there you have three tab stops to align the numbers, the units, and the ingredients.

Figure 32: Examples for use of tab stops. A) The right tab stop can be seen in the ruler on top. B) The right tab stop is used to align the numbers, the first left to align the units, and the second left to align the ingredients. Please note that the Show formatting feature is turned on.

A)
```
Onions:      →    2·oz¶
Potatoes:    →    1·lb¶
Beef:    →    1.5·lb¶
```

B)
```
10x·TBS¶
  → 500→mM → Tris¶
  → 1.5→M  →  NaCl¶
Adjust·pH·to·7.4·with·HCl¶
```

3. When working with headers and footers, tab stops can be used to have different pieces of information on the left, center, and right, or anywhere in between. For example, the name of the document could be left-aligned, "confidential" in the center and the page number on the right. The left tab is optional but the other two should be: a center tab in the center and a right tab on the right.

4. Now here's my favorite (and it's also scientific)! In fact, I think it is so useful, that I made an FAQ out of it (☞ FAQ 9 – Elaborate Tabs: How To Label A Gel Picture).

To align text at a tab stop simply press the `tab` *key (⬅➡), right? In general yes but it some cases no. So what are these exemptions?*

1. *When you press the* `tab` *key at the very beginning of a line of text (not an empty line) it will shift the first line indent to the next pre-defined tab stop.*

2. *Within a table, pressing the* `tab` *key simply selects the next cell or, at the end of a table, inserts a new row. Tab stops can still be used though; simply press* `ctrl+tab`.

3. *In a numbered list, pressing the* `tab` *key at the beginning of a line will change the numbering to the next lower level (same as clicking the increase indent button* ⬚*). Pressing* `shift+tab` *will change to the next higher level (same as clicking the decrease indent button* ⬚ *).*

FAQ 9 – Elaborate Tabs: How To Label A Gel Picture

What I want to show here is to demonstrate how to put labels on anything that has vertical lanes using tab stops. During most scientific theses it will happen that you have to label one kind of picture or the other, be it a Western Blot, an agarose or SDS-polyacrylamide gel etc. I haven't seen anyone so far who takes advantage of tab stops to aid in this endeavor. Instead, everyone presses the space bar until everything is "kind of" in place. There are some significant disadvantages with that method. For one, the alignment is never accurate. Then, if you have to change the font, font size or have to correct a number, everything will be out of alignment. To avoid this and to have the labels aligned nicely with the picture content, here's what I do; the final result can be seen in ☞Figure 33:

1. Create two empty lines of normal text.
2. Insert the picture of a gel "in line with text" (☞ Images, Graphics, Objects & Co., 6.a) into the second empty line. Alternatively, it can be inserted almost every other way. However, I recommend placing it inside a text box (also in line with text) if it needs to be moved around.
3. Move the cursor into the empty line above the graphic. Again, if you need to be more flexible you can insert a text box wide enough to span the entire picture and continue with the following steps *inside* that text box.
4. Select the center tab ⊥ from the tab selector button (one click when the left tab L is shown).
5. Hold down the Alt key and place the center tab stops in the horizontal ruler such that the appearing vertical line is in the middle of the gel lane.
6. Now enter the lane numbers in the line where you just set the tab stops and press the tab key (⇥) *before* each number.
7. Lastly, you will have to add a legend to give those numbers a meaning. The way in my opinion is to draw a text box left or right of the graphic (see ☞ Text boxes below). In this text box start a numbered list by typing 1. [space]. If desired, change the numbered list's format and you're done! You can also change the appearance of the text box itself, e.g. add a colored background or a different border.

I provided the document "gel_labels.docx" in the bonus archive to play around with.

FAQ 9 – Elaborate Tabs: How To Label A Gel Picture

Figure 33: Adding labels to a Western Blot picture. A) Setting the tab stops. B) The final result including the labels and the legend. If you don't like the position of the labels place them in a text box.

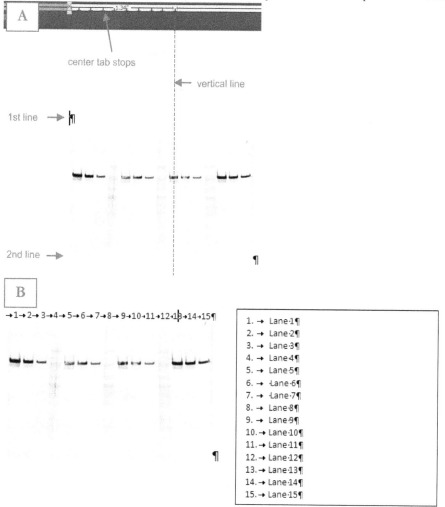

Text boxes

A text box is a moveable, sizeable, and very versatile element that allows you to position text and other object inside virtually anywhere inside the document. It is almost a small document if you wish. Word 2007 offers about 20 predefined text boxes for different occasions but you are still able to draw a plain old-fashioned text box. You can find the

text boxes in the Insert tab of the Ribbon inside the **Text** group. Click on the icon to open the selection; almost at the bottom you will find the option <u>D</u>raw **Text Box**. The last option (<u>S</u>ave Selection to Text Box Gallery) is only available if text has been selected. The selection will be saved in the text box gallery and can be used in the future.

As I mentioned, text boxes are like small documents in the actual document. That means you can format the text and paragraphs to your liking, insert graphic or other objects (only in line with text, ☞ Images, Graphics, Objects & Co.) and so on. The best thing is that you can move the text box around and position it as described earlier in ☞ Images, Graphics, Objects & Co..

Already have a paragraph (even including an in-line graphic or object) that you wish you had placed inside a text box? No problem! Select the everything and click on the <u>D</u>raw **Text Box** *option from the* Insert *tab/***Text** *section. The selected paragraph has been placed inside a text box automatically.*

Frames

Text boxes and frames are similar but have distinct features (copied from ☻ Microsoft Office Online):

Use frames when your text or graphics contain the following:

- *Comments (comment: A note or annotation that an author or reviewer adds to a document. Microsoft Word displays the comment in a balloon in the margin of the document or in the Reviewing Pane.), as indicated by comment marks (comment mark: Each time you add a comment to a document, Microsoft Word inserts a comment mark in the document. Comment marks appear when you click Markup on the View menu.).*
- *Footnotes or endnotes, as indicated by note reference marks (note reference mark: A number, character, or combination of characters that indicates that additional information is contained in a footnote or endnote.).*

- *Certain fields (field: A set of codes that instructs Microsoft Word to insert text, graphics, page numbers, and other material into a document automatically. For example, the DATE field inserts the current date.), including AUTONUM, AUTONUMLGL, AUTONUMOUT — used for numbering lists and paragraphs in legal documents and outlines — TC (Table of Contents Entry), TOC (Table of Contents), RD (Referenced Document), XE (Index Entry), TA (Table of Authorities Entry), and TOA (Table of Authority) fields.*

In other words, unless you want to use a small number of interactive fields you don't have to worry about it. As a rule of thumb, if you enter something in a text box and you cannot refer to content the way you want, try converting the text box into a frame.

Document Publication

Printing

Printing doesn't sound too difficult, does it? Just click the printer icon (that you have hopefully placed in your ☞ Quick Access Toolbar by now!) and a few minutes later you will have the results. Most of the time this is absolutely correct! There is not much to tell you about printing but there are a few tips that might improve the process and save a few trees.

Print Preview

You might be wondering why I start with the Print Preview option. This option, available through the Print Dialog described below, is much more important than you might think. Not only will it give you an idea of how your document will look like. In my opinion the most critical aspect is that your fields are updated and you will be able to see if there are any hidden differences between your on-screen document and the actual printed version. So take the time to critically assess the results in Print Preview before wasting paper!

The Print dialog

There are three ways to get to the Print dialog:

1. 🗂 → <u>P</u>rint

2. Ctrl+P

3. Or place the Preview and Print button into the Quick Access Toolbar (☞ Figure 34).
   Careful! If you add the wrong button (Quick Print) like most, printing will begin immediately after you clicked the icon and not open the Print menu!

Figure 34: The Preview and Print button, a very helpful addition to the Quick Access Toolbar.

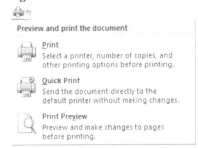

Either option will take you to the Print dialog as shown in ☞ Figure 35. Obviously, you will only see the printers that you have installed on your computer. This is also the reason why I will not go into details what the <u>P</u>roperties button will show; it will open another dialog where you can adjust settings that are specific for the selected printer.

Figure 35: The Print dialog not only lets you change which printer to use but also offers a lot of other helpful options.

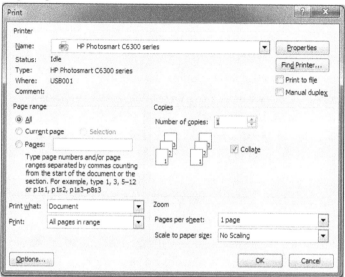

What you want to do first is to check if the correct printer is selected (<u>N</u>ame: drop-down menu); this is especially important when printing from a computer that is connected to multiple printers (e.g. networked). Underneath the drop-down menu you will find current information about the printer.

Next you have to select what parts of the document you want to print. Default is to print all pages. The other options that you have are:

- Curr<u>e</u>nt page: Prints the page where the cursor is located and NOT the currently visible page.
- <u>S</u>election (only available when content was selected prior): Will print only the selected content. *Note: The position on the paper hardly ever is the same as in the document.*
- Pa<u>g</u>es: Classically, people type in only the page numbers or combinations thereof (e.g. 1-5; 1, 4,5; etc.). This works great. But did you know that you can also print ☞ section-specific pages? It is actually described just underneath the text field: p1s1, p1s2 etc. What this means is you will print the first page (p1) from the first section (s1) or the first page (p1) from the second section (s2). Very cool, huh? Not sure where to find what section you are in? Check the tip ☞ above where sections are explained.

Very closely related to these options is the P<u>r</u>int: drop-down menu. Here you can specify that you might just want to print odd or even pages. Very helpful if you want to print manual duplex!

You will probably rarely need to change the selection from the Print <u>w</u>hat: drop-down. Still I want to briefly explain what you can change here:

- All pages in range: Yep, exactly that.
- Document showing markup: This will print the document but also comments and track changes. *This will be the default setting when the document contains comments!*
- List of markup: Will print just the markup as a list.
- Styles: Prints an overview of all used styles including the specifications.
- Building Blocks entries: When you set building blocks (not described in this book) you can print the information using this selection.
- Key assignments: If you assigned key shortcuts to for example styles this will print a list of your customized key assignments.

If you need more than one copy you can select more. The default setting for more than one copy is to collate the print-outs, meaning that first one set is printed, then the next. If you uncheck this option, each page will be printed multiple times, then the next.

If you want to save paper or need to change the print layout, the Zoom options might be helpful. You can select how many pages you want to print on one side of the sheet or to what paper size you want to fit the document. *Note: You will specify duplex settings, i.e. double-sided printing, in the printer-specific* <u>P</u>roperties *dialog.*

Publishing As PDF

In these days nobody really uses Word or other editable text documents anymore after they have been finalized. If you distribute a (editable) Word file others might not have the right fonts installed, their printer setup is different and messes up the page layout and so on. Distributing your thesis as a PDF (portable document format) document allows recipients to display and print it independent of the computer platform they use. If you have the right program (e.g. 🌍 Adobe Professional) you can even restrict what others can do with the document, for example they cannot print or copy text from it.

Using Word's PDF Function

Before Microsoft implemented the Save as… PDF/XPS plug-in as standard a third-party program was required to convert a Word document into PDF. Luckily this is in the past now. If your Office suite does not show this feature you should download the latest updates! I found that Word still knows the most about what is going on internally and using the built-in PDF converter gives me the least trouble. Try it: → Save <u>As</u>... → <u>P</u>DF or XPS

This will open a dialog very similar to the regular **Save** dialog where you can specify where and under what name to safe the PDF file. When you click on the **Options...** button you can choose from a few options to modify the PDF (☞ Figure 36). Some options are reminiscent of the Print dialog (☞ Figure 35). More important than what pages to export might be the way the structure of the Word document will be reflected in the PDF file. I highly recommend selecting the features as shown in ☞ Figure 36. This will convert all heading to bookmarks that will be displayed in the PDF reader. Cross-references and hyperlinks will also still be working.

Figure 36: The Save As PDF options allow to change a few export options.

Third Party Software

As a general note, many PDF converters work like a printer and do not export neat features like cross-references or hyperlinks. There are tons of free programs out there and I suggest everyone finds out what they think works best. A lot of websites offer free online conversions as well.

I have Adobe Professional 9 installed and when I exported this book using the Adobe PDF plug-in I noticed some weird artifacts so I decided to simply go with the Word built-in function. However, when it comes to editing the created PDF Adobe Pro is fantastic. You can add, extract, rotate, and delete pages, create a portfolio of different files, save forms with data and much more. I am sure there are cheaper alternatives out there but I got a pretty sweet deal!

Using the Keyboard

I will not teach you how to use all 10 fingers to type and get 150 hits per minute. This section will introduce you to what else you can do with the keyboard besides simply typing words. Using keyboard shortcuts is not only very quick but studies have also shown that switching less between mouse and keyboard may be beneficial for your health:

- Kill Your Mouse - Use Keyboard Shortcuts (http://longevity.about.com/od/longevitytools/a/mouse_rsi.htm);

- ERGONOMIC KEYBOARD SHORTCUTS (http://www.ehs.ucsf.edu/Ergonomics/oehsErgoKeyboardShortcuts.asp);

- Interventions for the primary prevention of work-related carpal tunnel syndrome (http://www.ncbi.nlm.nih.gov/pubmed/10793280).

General Windows Keyboard Shortcuts

Below (☞ Table 6) is a list of the most important keyboard shortcuts that come built-in with Microsoft Windows. *Note: Not all listed shortcuts will work with all Windows versions.*

Table 6: **General Windows keyboard shortcuts.** Not all shortcuts might be available in all Windows versions.

Keyboard shortcut	Action
ctrl+C; ctrl+Insert	Copies the selected file, text, object etc. into the Clipboard
ctrl+X; Shift+Delete	Copies the selected file, text, object etc. into the Clipboard and removes it from its original position
ctrl+V; Shift+Insert	Pastes the last copied item of the Clipboard
ctrl+Z	Undoes the last action; not always available
ctrl+A	Selects all files, text, or objects in the active window; might be overridden by specific programs
ctrl+Home	Jumps to the first position of a list or text
ctrl+End	Jumps to the last position of a list or text
Alt+F4	Closes the active window
Alt+tab	Toggles between open windows
F1	Commonly used to display a help window
⊞+F	Opens the Search window or ⓖ Google desktop if installed
⊞+E	Opens the Windows explorer window
⊞+L	Locks the computer and requires to log in again
⊞+D	Switches to the desktop (all open windows are minimized); pressing it again restores the previous configuration
⊞+M	Minimizes all open windows

Word-Specific Keyboard Shortcuts

You will find that most of the shortcuts that were defined for Windows will work the same way in most programs. Many programs will offer a lot more shortcuts that are specific to the functions of the actual program. In ☞ Table 7 below I listed the most important (default) keyboard shortcuts for Microsoft Word 2007. I hope that you also will be able to navigate through and edit your document much faster once you get used to using keyboard shortcuts!

Table 7: Microsoft Word 2007 keyboard shortcuts. They will help you save a lot of time and relax your "mouse hand". You should add your own shortcuts!

Keyboard shortcut	Action
Selection shortcuts	
ctrl+Shift+←	Highlights the entire word left of the cursor
ctrl+Shift+→	Highlights the entire word right of the cursor
ctrl+Shift+↑	Highlights all text from the cursor to the beginning of the paragraph
ctrl+Shift+↓	Highlights all text from the cursor to the end of the paragraph
ctrl+Shift+Home	Highlights text from cursor to the beginning of the document
ctrl+Shift+End	Highlights text from cursor to the end of the document
Movement shortcuts	
ctrl+←	Jumps to the beginning of the word left of the cursor
ctrl+→	Jumps to the end of the word or beginning of the next
ctrl+↑	Jumps to the beginning of the paragraph
ctrl+↓	Jumps to the beginning of the paragraph
ctrl+PageUp	Jumps to the beginning of the previous page
ctrl+PageDown	Jumps to the beginning of the next paragraph
ctrl+Home	Jumps to the beginning of the document
ctrl+End	Jumps to the end of the document
Dialog shortcuts	
ctrl+K	Opens the dialog for hyperlinks
ctrl+D	Opens the Font format dialog
ctrl+H	Opens the Find/Replace dialog
Document shortcuts	
Alt	Shows shortcuts for Ribbon and Quick Access Toolbar
ctrl+F4	Closes the active document but keeps Word open
ctrl+O	Lets you select a file to open
ctrl+S	Lets you choose a location and file name for saving (new document) or quick save (edited document)
ctrl+P	Opens the Print dialog
ctrl+	

Keyboard shortcut	Action
Formatting shortcuts	
ctrl+U	Underlines the selected text
ctrl+I	Italicizes the selected text
ctrl+B	Makes the selected text bold
ctrl+=	Formats the selected text as subscript
ctrl++	Formats the selected text as superscript
ctrl+Enter	Inserts a page break
ctrl+1 (2, 3)	Formats the active paragraph as Heading 1 (2, 3)
Character shortcuts	
ctrl+Shift+space	Inserts a protected space that will keep adjacent characters together
ctrl+-	Inserts an optional hyphen where that long words will be hyphenated
ctrl+Shift+-	Inserts a protected dash that will not be used as hyphen, i.e. adjacent characters remains in one line
Character shortcuts	
F9	Will update the field code when cursor is placed in a field; otherwise no effect
Alt+F9	Toggle field codes; will display the field code instead of the result
ctrl+A;F9	Updates all field codes in the document; NOTE: fields in header and footer will not be updated

As I described earlier where I talked about ☞ Styles you can and should create customized keyboard shortcuts to facilitate your writing process. As a suggestion, either format Headings 1-3 to your liking (e.g. in a ☞ template for your thesis) or add separate styles for your own headings and associate the ctrl+1 (2, 3) shortcuts with them.

Mouse Gestures

Obviously I don't want to condemn the use of the mouse completely! It is very helpful but just like the keyboard shortcuts, mouse gestures are not used to their full potential. I provided only a short list of mouse gestures (☞ Table 8) since I have not found many at all.

Table 8: A list of the most important mouse gestures in Word 2007.

Mouse gesture	Action
ctrl+left-click	Selects the entire sentence
Alt+right-click	Opens the Research bar (online content)
Shift+right-click in table	Selects the entire column
ctrl+wheel up	Zoom in
ctrl+wheel down	Zoom out
Right-click just left of a table	Selects the entire row
Right-click in text	Opens a context menu with specific options
Double-click	Selects the entire word
Triple-click	Selects the entire paragraph
Drag and drop	Moves the selected text or objects to new position; if the ctrl key is pressed simultaneously a copy will be created

Contact

Questions? Comments? Praise? Suggestions? Whatever it is that bothers you with this book or my website (http://academia-nutcrackers.com), I would like to know! The way I work is "As long as I don't know that something is wrong, I won't change anything!" So if you can think of anything that might improve this book or the website please tell me and I will work on it!

Contact Details

Email: support@academia-nutcrackers.com

eForm: http://academia-nutcrackers.com/contact-form

Skype: funnycreature-usa

Table of Figures

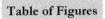

www.ingramcontent.com/pod-product-compliance
Lightning Source LLC
Chambersburg PA
CBHW060455060326
40689CB00020B/4537